Storybooks
for
Tough Times

Storybooks
for
Tough Times

Laura Ann Campbell

fulcrum resources
Golden, Colorado

Library of Congress Cataloging-in-Publication Data

Campbell, Laura Ann.
    Storybooks for tough times / by Laura Ann Campbell.
       p.   cm.
    Includes bibliographical references and indexes.
    ISBN 1-55591-964-2 (alk. paper)
    1. Children's stories, American—Bibliography. 2. Social problems—Juvenile fiction
Bibliography. 3. Bibliotherapy for children—United States Bibliography. 4. Children—
Books and reading—United States. I. Title.
Z1037.C178 1999
[PS374.C454]
016.813'540809282—dc21   99–16278
                                                CIP

Printed in the United States of America
0 9 8 7 6 5 4 3 2 1

Cover illustration © copyright 1999 by K. Michael Crawford

Fulcrum Publishing
350 Indiana Street, Suite 350
Golden, Colorado 80401-5093
(800) 992-2908 • (303) 277-1623
www.fulcrum-resources.com

*To Carolyn and Tanner, who bring joy and peace
to my life and delight to my days.*

Contents

Acknowledgments

When asked about the book I was writing, I was always quick to point out that my task was not about writing children's stories but rather sharing some of the amazing array of children's books created by others. To the authors and illustrators whose works are cited herein and to those whose works I have yet to discover, thank you for bringing your talents to the world of children's literature and for providing adults and children with some light during their troubled times. To Suzanne Barchers, whose confidence in my abilities far exceeded my own, thank you for your guidance, encouragement, and friendship over the years. Your strength as an author, mentor, and friend provides support and inspiration in so many things I do. Marty, I will keep it simple: thank you. To Shawn and Jen, your friendship and support mean so much—thank you for always being there for me. To the friends and families who shared their favorite books and encouraged me to keep going, even after endless trips to the library and hours on the computer, thank you for believing in me. Finally, to Bobby, Carolyn, and Tanner, who gave me the time and space to complete this project—your love transcends all.

Introduction

As the mother of two young children I find myself frequently searching for answers to their never-ending questions: why do cars go fast? Why can't I go to school too (even though I'm only two)? When will it be Christmas? Will you get me that for my birthday? These, and many of their questions, have answers that if not immediately logical to four-and seven-year-old minds, at least satisfy their curiosity and quiet their queries.

But then, there are the questions that make me stop in my tracks, take a quick breath, and roll through the years of accumulated wisdom that comes with growing up and raising a family. Why is Aunt Mary's hair falling out? Why does Ron have to move? Why can't Grandpa hear me very well? Why did Mrs. Gordon die? The answers to these questions are not simple and cannot be formulated quickly.

These are the kinds of questions parents, teachers, therapists, and others who care about and for children are faced with, and the questions seem to increase as children begin exploring the world beyond their front door. The more children are exposed to the beauty, wonder, intrigue—and mystery—of their world, the more they grow and develop minds to seek answers.

Storybooks for Tough Times seeks to provide adults with ways of leading children to stories that will help them begin to deal with or understand the "tough times" of life. Each chapter deals with a different issue or topic that may generate questions in the mind of a child, and includes picture books that adults and children can read together to begin answering those questions. Each book listing includes the author, title, publishing company, and publication date so that it can be easily accessed at libraries or bookstores. A brief summary of each book is followed by connections to life issues and discussion questions to help adults in their effort to comfort and guide children around these difficult issues.

Children's questions never diminish in number and seem to grow in their complexity as they get older. When questions of life loom in the mind of a child, solace and answers can often be found in the comfort of a book with familiar characters and simple storylines. *Storybooks for Tough Times* seeks to be a resource for adults seeking some answers for children.

CHAPTER 1:

Abuse

Chilly Stomach
by Jeannette Franklin Caines

Laurie Tells
by Linda Lowery

Daisy
by E. Sandy Powell

Chilly Stomach

Caines, Jeannette Franklin. 1986. *Chilly Stomach*.
Illustrated by Pat Cummings. New York: Harper & Row.

Story Summary

Chilly Stomach describes the feelings a little girl has when her Uncle Jim comes to visit and tickles her, kisses her, and hugs her. It's a different feeling from when her mom and dad hug her, and she wishes Uncle Jim wouldn't come for dinner every Saturday. Whenever her Uncle Jim spends the night, she asks to spend the night at her friend Jill's house. Jill has an uncle who hugs and kisses too, but it doesn't give her a chilly stomach. Knowing only that she feels different when her uncle hugs her, she confides in her friend—convincing her to tell her parents. Though she is frightened of what they will say or do, or that they won't believe her, she decides in the end that she wants them to know.

Making Connections

Physical abuse by an adult can evoke feelings of confusion and guilt in a child. Understanding what is appropriate and what is not appropriate touching and what to do if they are abused will provide children with a way to stop the abuse.

Discussion Questions

- Do you know someone who has been physically abused?
- Do you know the difference between good and bad touching?
- What would you do if an adult were abusing you?

Laurie Tells

Lowery, Linda. 1994. *Laurie Tells*.
Illustrated by John Eric Karpinski. Minneapolis, Minn.: Carolrhoda.

Story Summary

Laurie takes a walk and thinks about how it used to be before her dad began to touch her inappropriately. She wonders how hands that used to push her in swings or button her coat could now be too big and too touchy. She reflects on how she tried to tell her mother a year ago, but that her mother didn't seem to hear her. Finally she decides her aunt would understand. In a painful conversation, Laurie tells her aunt what has happened. Her aunt comforts her and arranges for her to stay with her, reassuring her that she will find someone who knows what they should do next.

Making Connections

This book shows how a youngster faces the reality of telling an adult about her experiences. The clear writing from Laurie's point of view shows the struggle involved, while emphasizing the need to find a trusted adult to tell of the sexual abuse.

Discussion Questions

- Have you ever had a hard time telling someone something painful?
- What helped you with the process?
- Can you think of strategies, such as writing down your thoughts first, that might have helped Laurie talk to her aunt?

Daisy

Powell, E. Sandy. 1991. *Daisy*.
Illustrated by Peter J. Thornton. Minneapolis, Minn.: Carolrhoda.

Story Summary

Told from the perspective of Daisy, a nine-year-old girl who recounts her story of abuse, this story reveals the ways a child mentally and emotionally protects herself from an abusive father. Daisy would use her walk home from school to "collect pictures" in her mind and transfer those images to paper if she had time to draw before going to bed. Referring to her home as the "ogre's castle," Daisy shares that because she had trouble breathing at home she would suck in "air between my teeth, saving up extra for the night." Throughout the story Daisy tells of life with her father, including cooking and cleaning for him— and trying to protect herself from him when he called her names, broke things in anger, kicked her, and slapped her. She lives with her secret for a long time until her new friend, a tutor at school, notices her bruises. Things get even worse at home when Daisy's dad loses his job. The tutor finally shares with Daisy that she, too, was the victim of abuse, and that after she told an adult about what happened she and her father got the important help they needed. In the end, Daisy is brave enough to say what her father did to her, and she goes to live with a foster family near the school.

Making Connections

Frightened and confused, children who are abused are frequently unable to share with anyone the pain they are experiencing. Helping them face their fears and understand that they can confide in and trust an adult will help them see a way out of their suffering.

Discussion Questions

- Do you know someone who has been hurt by an adult? How did it make you feel?

- What can you do if an adult is hurting you?

CHAPTER 2:

Adoption

A Family for Jamie
An Adoption Story
by Suzanne Bloom

Tell Me Again About the Night I Was Born
by Jamie Lee Curtis

A Mother for Choco
by Keiko Kasza

The Day We Met You
by Phoebe Koehler

Did My First Mother Love Me?
A Story for an Adopted Child
by Kathryn Ann Miller

A Family for Jamie
An Adoption Story

Bloom, Suzanne. 1991. *A Family for Jamie: An Adoption Story.*
New York: Crown.

Story Summary

In Jamie's family everybody likes to make things: towers of blocks, cakes and cookies, and funny stories at bedtime. Jamie's mom and dad liked to make things before he came to live with them too, but the one thing they could not make was a baby. They wished for a child who could eat the cookies and paint the birdhouses they made and play with the blocks and other fun toys they wanted to have in their home, and on whom they could shower lots of love and attention. Colorfully illustrated, *A Family for Jamie* begins with the story of two people who go through a lengthy adoption process that includes interviews, visits from the adoption agency, and the passing of many seasons before they finally get their baby. Friends and relatives who bring diapers, clothes, toys, and much love to the new family share their joy.

Making Connections

Learning about adoption and realizing one has been adopted pose many questions and comments that make responding difficult. Helping children understand that adopted children can receive as much love and care from parents and siblings as biological children, and that many parents work very hard to adopt their children, is a story well told in this book.

Discussion Questions

- Do you understand what it means to be adopted?

- Would you like to learn about how you came to be adopted?

- Does it make you feel different from other children that you are adopted? How?

Tell Me Again
About the Night I Was Born

Curtis, Jamie Lee. 1996. *Tell Me Again About the Night I Was Born.*
Illustrated by Laura Cornell. New York: HarperCollins.

Story Summary

A little girl asks her parents to tell her again about that special night when she was born. She reviews how the phone rang in the middle of the night and how they got on an airplane to get her. She asks to hear again about how her parents couldn't grow her themselves, so they adopted her from a young mother. She talks about the many firsts: first diaper, first bottle, and first lullaby. This overview of those special first days of adoption are brightened with humorous, simple, color illustrations that youngsters will enjoy repeatedly.

Making Connections

Adopted children understand the process at different levels throughout their growing-up years. Young children need to know the basics, such as this narrative provides. As they grow older, they can hear and understand more details. This book demonstrates how necessary it is to repeat the story of adoption.

Discussion Questions

- Can you remember things that you did first with your adoptive parents?
- What special items do you have, such as the "Me" book shown in this story?
- How were you perfect? Did you have ten perfect toes too?

A Mother for Choco

Kasza, Keiko. 1992. *A Mother for Choco*.
New York: Putnam.

Story Summary

Choco is a little bird who lives all alone and wishes he had a mother. He sets out to look for one, meeting all kinds of creatures who tell him they can't be his mother because they aren't like him. The giraffe, the penguins, the walrus, and the elephant don't look like him and can't be his mother. When Choco runs into Mrs. Bear, he knows she can't be his mother because she, too, does not look like him, but he accepts her offers of comfort anyway. Asking what his mommy would do for him, Choco tells Mrs. Bear she would hold him tight, give him kisses, sing and dance, and cheer him up. Mrs. Bear offers to do all those things for Choco and to be his mother, even though she doesn't look like him, and takes him home to live with her other children. Hippy the hippopotamus, Ally the alligator, and Piggy the pig are all happy to have another brother around. Mrs. Bear gives all her children lots of hugs and love—and Choco discovers he is very happy his new mommy looks just the way she does.

Making Connections

Understanding the complexities of adoption can often be better done for young children when dramatized by animals with human qualities. Choco's search for a mother leads him to ask many of the same questions other adopted children may ask and provides an opportunity for children to begin to get some of the answers.

Discussion Questions

- How are you different from your parents, brothers and sisters, and other family members?

- In what ways are you like the other members of your family?

- What is it about the members of your family that make them special to you?

- What are the special things about you that your family loves?

The Day We Met You

Koehler, Phoebe. 1990. *The Day We Met You.*
New York: Bradbury.

Story Summary

In minimal text and simple words, the story of one child's adoption is accompanied by full-page illustrations done in soft pastels. New parents tell the story of what it was like on the day they met their adopted child. On a bright sunny day, they went to the hospital to meet their new child. They borrowed a car seat for the ride home, and bought plenty of bottles and formula so the baby would have enough to eat. They purchased diapers, pajamas, and clothes so the baby would have enough to wear, and a mobile full of elephants so the baby would have fun things to look at in her crib. Other family members were happy the new baby was coming home too, including Grandpa, who brought a teddy bear. A friend brought a quilt to keep the baby warm, and a neighbor brought a cradle so the baby could sleep. With their hearts full of love, the new parents brought their baby home and felt like the sun was shining inside of them.

Making Connections

Understanding the love and joy that goes into preparing for a new baby helps adopted children realize they are loved as much as biological children. Especially for very young children, this book provides the beginnings of understanding of adoption and presents a warm and loving look at how much parents prepare.

Discussion Questions

- How do you feel about being adopted? Do you know what the day was like when your parents first met you?

- What can you say to other children when they ask you about being adopted?

- Who are the special people in your life that love you, talk to you, or visit with you?

Did My First Mother Love Me?
A Story for an Adopted Child
Miller, Kathryn Ann. 1994.
Did My First Mother Love Me? A Story for an Adopted Child.
Illustrated by Jami Moffett.
Buena Park, Calif.: Morning Glory.

Story Summary

Morgan often wonders about her birth mother, and whether she loved her or not. Her mom proves that her birth mother did love her by showing Morgan the letter her birth mother wrote when she was born. In it she explains how her love grew for the baby inside her as the baby grew, too. Counting the weeks and days until the baby would be born, Morgan's birth mother thought of all the things she wished for the baby in the future, and her wish that she could give her baby all those things. Realizing that her wish would not come true, she gives the precious gift of a baby to Morgan's parents to care for and love. With a special section for parents about talking with children about adoption, this story offers many resources for families seeking answers to adoption questions.

Making Connections

One of the most commonly asked set of questions children have about being adopted deals with their biological parents. In addition to the simple story that conveys for children what one mother experienced, this book provides additional information for parents.

Discussion Questions
- Do you understand the difference between your mom and your birth mother?
- In what ways are you like your parents? In what ways are you different?

CHAPTER 3:

Aging

Some Fine Grampa!
by Alan Arkin

The Memory Box
by Mary Bahr

Grandpa's Teeth
by Rod Clement

Great-Uncle Alfred Forgets
by Ben Schecter

Some Fine Grampa!

Arkin, Alan. 1994. *Some Fine Grampa!*
Illustrated by Dirk Zimmer. New York: HarperCollins.

Story Summary

Grampa comes to live with Molly and her parents. Molly's mother tells her that his mind is starting to wander. When he arrives, he has trouble with some basic skills, such as wearing his shorts on his head instead of a hat. He also tells Molly some seemingly outrageous stories about gorillas he lived with, a polar bear that knits, giant robots that could tap dance, and so forth. Finally Molly's parents decide he needs more supervision, and they build an apartment for him and hire a lady to care for him. He refuses to let the caretaker into his apartment, locking himself in for a week. But when his birthday comes, he lets Molly and her parents come to the party. The surprise ending, complete with all the friends he has talked about, shows that Grampa's stories were not so outrageous after all.

Making Connections

Having an aging grandparent in the house can put stress on the family. It can be easy to dismiss their stories as exaggerations or as developing out of confusion. This story encourages respecting previous experiences and tolerating differences.

Discussion Questions

- Do you know any elderly people?
- Do they like to tell stories about their earlier experiences?
- Can you listen to and enjoy their stories?
- Is it sometimes hard to tell what is true and what may be fantasy?
- Could all of this story be true?
- Does it matter if it isn't true?
- Would you like to know this grandpa?

The Memory Box

Bahr, Mary. 1992. *The Memory Box.*
Illustrated by David Cunningham. Morton Grove, Ill.: Albert Whitman.

Story Summary

Zach has spent many summers with his grandparents at their home on the lake, fishing with Gramps and eating Gram's good cooking. This summer starts out no different as he looks forward to catching walleye on the lake and cleaning them with the special knife Gramps uses. Something changes, however, when Gramps suggests they make a Memory Box, full of special things and notes of special times. The reason for the box is unclear to Zach until Gram explains that Gramps has Alzheimer's. It's hard for Zach to know exactly what the disease means until he sees the results—Gramps forgets to shave one day, Zach hears him talking to someone who isn't there, and he wanders into a patch of poison ivy—from which Zach must lead him out. It becomes clear just how difficult the disease is when Gram awakens Zach one morning and asks him to go find Gramps who has wandered off without his shoes. Zach finds him sitting on a hill in the woods, with tears in his eyes, because he got lost and couldn't remember how to get home. Zach tries to understand what is happening and comes to realize that Gramps will continue to get worse—but also realizes how he can help Gramps and cherish the memories they create in the Memory Box.

Making Connections

Alzheimer's can be a difficult and frightening disease for children to face when they realize nothing they can do will help someone they love. Learning how to understand the changes and accept their inevitability will better enable children to deal with the situation.

Discussion Questions

- In what ways have you noticed Alzheimer's changing someone you love?
- What can you do to help him or her feel better?
- What special memories do you have of being with him or her?

Grandpa's Teeth

Clement, Rod. 1997. *Grandpa's Teeth*.
New York: HarperCollins.

Story Summary

Calamity strikes when Grandpa's teeth, handmade by the finest Swiss craftsmen, disappear. In this humorous, illustrated mystery, everyone works with the police to discover who would steal the teeth. To allay suspicion, everyone smiles broadly to show that they have their own teeth, not the missing ones. Finally, the whole town decides they have to work together to replace the teeth. They take up a collection and give both Grandpa and another elderly resident new teeth.

Making Connections

Seeing false teeth in a glass or seeing an aging grandparent without teeth can be frightening to a child. Similarly, signs of the aging process, such as losing teeth or becoming deaf, can be confusing. This slightly outrageous story approaches aging lightly.

Discussion Questions

- Have you lost your first set of teeth yet?
- How can you lose other teeth?
- Have you ever seen someone's false teeth?
- What would it be like to no longer have your teeth?
- What other things might happen to your body as you get old?
- How can you help someone who has lost teeth or who is losing the ability to hear?

Great-Uncle Alfred Forgets

Schecter, Ben. 1996. *Great-Uncle Alfred Forgets.*
New York: HarperCollins.

Story Summary

Emily and Great-Uncle Alfred visit while they trim the Christmas tree. Great-Uncle Alfred needs help finding his shoes and seems confused about what the season is. They go for a walk and Great-Uncle Alfred continues to show his confusion while they talk. Emily shows patience, asking him to tell her a story. As he reminisces, Emily enjoys their time together.

Making Connections

Conversation can be difficult with an older person whose mind seems to wander. In this sensitive portrayal, Emily intuitively knows that sometimes a conversation does not need to be logical. She encourages her Great-Uncle Alfred to connect with her, enjoying the companionship.

Discussion Questions

- Do you know someone who is very old?
- Does that person always understand what is happening, or does the person sometimes seem confused?
- What can you do with a person who acts confused?
- What was special about Emily's relationship with her Great-Uncle Alfred?
- How can you develop a special relationship with an elderly person?

Heaven

Allan, Nicholas. 1996. *Heaven*.
New York: HarperCollins.

Story Summary

Lily wakes up one morning to find her dog Dill packing his suitcase. When she asks where he is going, he points to the sky and says, "Up there." He slowly leads her to understand that she can't come with him and he can't stay to play because the angels have come to take him to heaven. When she tries to convince him that he won't like it, Dill asks her to imagine what it might be like—and she realizes it could be a place that is nice, but different, for everyone. Lily finds herself upset that Dill is leaving her, and reminds him that he might be going down because of all the bad things he did. Dill acknowledges he did some bad things, but confidently predicts he will go up. When the angels tell him its time to leave, Dill says good-bye, and Lily goes home to Dill's empty bed, leash, and food bowl. Her sadness is heavy, but is lifted when a stray dog becomes her friend and helps her learn to love again.

Making Connections

Though the death of a person or pet is typically not as predictable as portrayed in this story, it can still serve as an opportunity for children to understand death and its finality.

Discussion Questions

- Who have you known in your life who has died? How did it make you feel?

- What do you think happens after people and animals die?

- What can you do to help yourself feel better when you are sad?

Someday a Tree

Bunting, Eve. 1993. *Someday a Tree*.
Illustrated by Ronald Himler. New York: Clarion.

Story Summary

Alice and her mom visit the big tree across the meadow every day. Its large trunk and long branches hold many leaves that provide shade for them and the strangers who often stop for a picnic. During one of their visits Alice notices that the ground around the tree has a strange odor to it and that the grass is turning yellow. The tree doctor is called who, after examining the leaves and soil, concludes someone has unloaded poison near the tree and that it is dying. Alice and her family and neighbors from town do their best to help it survive—they put in fresh soil and protect it from the sun with large nets, and some people even leave get-well cards and chicken soup. Nothing works, however, and they accept that they are too late to save the tree. Alice feels as her mother does—distraught that someone could do something so horrible to cause a big, beautiful tree to die. As Alice tries to cope with the concept of death, she remembers the acorns she collected when the tree was healthy. She wakes early one morning and goes outside to plant her acorns, reflecting on the life she is able to provide, even in the shadow of death.

Making Connections

Encountering death for the first time is a difficult experience for children. Sharing with them how things and people die and how life for others continues, will help them better understand their feelings.

Discussion Questions

- How did you feel when you found out someone or something you loved had died?
- What can you do to keep the memory of that person or thing alive in your heart?

Bye, Mis' Lela

Carter, Dorothy. 1998. *Bye, Mis' Lela*.
Illustrated by Harvey Stevenson. New York: Farrar, Straus & Giroux.

Story Summary

A little girl stays with Mis' Lela when her mother goes to work. She enjoys Mis' Lela's animals, yard, and special visitors, such as Mr. Tinker Man or Mis' Bible Lady. When Mis' Lela dies, the girl's mother takes her to the wake. The grown-ups talk about how she's now resting with the Comforter. The girl says good-bye to Mis' Lela, while talking with her mother about how Mis' Lela seems to be sleeping. Later, when she is big enough to go to school, she walks by Mis' Lela's house and greets her, just as if she still were there.

Making Connections

This simple story gives the reader basic information about what happens when someone dies. The mother draws a parallel to a long, long sleep, but makes it clear that Mis' Lela can't hear, eat, see, or dream. The finality of death is tempered with the ongoing memory of her life through the young girl.

Discussion Questions?

- Have you ever known an older person who died?
- Did you go to the wake? What was it like?
- Did the girl forget Mis' Lela?
- How can you keep the memory of a loved person alive?

Nana Upstairs & Nana Downstairs

dePaola, Tomie. 1973. *Nana Upstairs & Nana Downstairs*.
New York: G. P. Putnam's Sons.

Story Summary

When Tommy was a little boy, he and his family would go to visit his grandmother and great-grandmother every week. His great-grandmother was always in bed upstairs from where his grandmother was cooking, so he called them Nana Upstairs and Nana Downstairs. He enjoyed spending time with his great-grandmother and loved it when she let him get candy off her dresser. They would sit together and talk, take naps together, and eat together. Tommy thought she was beautiful. When Tommy is told that Nana Upstairs has died, he tries to understand why and feels very sad. A falling star that he sees out his window at night makes him feel better, and he decides it is a kiss sent from heaven from Nana Upstairs. When his grandmother dies many years later, he sees another falling star—and thinks of them both as Nana Upstairs.

Making Connections

Children lucky enough to know and spend time with their great-grandparents learn about families but often must learn to deal with death at a relatively young age. This story provides young children with a simple sense of understanding of what death means.

Discussion Questions

- Who have you known in your life who's died? How did it make you feel?
- What special memories do you have with that person?
- What things can you do that will help you remember that person?

Beautiful

Fowler, Susie Gregg. 1998. *Beautiful.*
Illustrated by Jim Fowler. New York: Greenwillow.

Story Summary

Uncle George's birthday gift to a young boy includes a variety of seeds and planting equipment. They work together to start a garden. Uncle George tells the boy that he is going away for a while because he is sick. As the garden grows, they communicate by phone and postcards. Finally Uncle George returns, but he is near death. The young boy brings a beautiful bouquet to his bed, and they celebrate the garden together.

Making Connections

This story demonstrates how thoughtfully a loved one can prepare another for death. Teaching a young person a beloved activity is a testament to powerful connections that can endure beyond the ending of the relationship. Use this to help older children think about what they gain from people who have touched their lives.

Discussion Questions

- Uncle George gave this boy a great gift when he began a garden with him. Do you know people who have taught you special skills?

- What do you miss about favorite relatives or friends who have died?

- What activities did you share?

- How can you keep their memories alive?

My Grandfather's Hat

Scheller, Melanie. 1992. *My Grandfather's Hat.*
Illustrated by Keiko Narahashi. New York: Maxwell Macmillan International.

Story Summary

Whenever Jason saw his grandfather he always had his brown hat. During one visit Jason's grandfather forgets to hang up his hat and Jason squashes it when he jumps on the sofa. Jason's mom is angry with him, but Grandma and Grandpa explain it is a tough hat and has been through a lot. His grandfather bought the hat long before Jason was born, and he would lift it off his head when greeting people on the street. Grandpa put the hat on top of a snowman's head, and made a mess when an egg he carried in it broke—he just wiped it clean and put it back on his head. After Jason's grandfather dies Dad talks about the memories they will always have of Grandpa, even though he is no longer with them. Mom tells Jason to be careful with the hat after Grandma gives it to him, but Grandma says there's nothing Jason could do to the hat that hadn't already happened. Jason decides that though it's too big now, he will cherish it always and wear it proudly when he is older.

Making Connections

Remembering people we love by holding onto things they owned and treasured is one way children can cope with the loss of a grandparent, parent, or special friend.

Discussion Questions

- What memories do you have of someone you loved who has died?
- What special things do you have that remind you of them?

Saying Good-bye to Grandma

Thomas, Jane Resh. 1988. *Saying Good-bye to Grandma*.
Illustrated by Marcia Sewall. New York: Clarion.

Story Summary

Seven-year-old Suzi and her family gather with her cousins and aunts and uncles when Grandma dies. This story explains rituals of death shared by one family. Mom and Dad share their memories of Grandma, and Suzi notices Mom looking out the window and blowing her nose a lot. Everyone pitches in to help with dinner, and though the kids talk and eat, the adults are very quiet. Suzi goes to talk to her Grandpa who is standing alone on the dock one night, and he tells her how Grandma liked to watch the sun set and catch and cook fish. She hears Grandpa crying in his room one night and worries because Grandpa won't eat. At the funeral parlor they will say good-bye to Grandma, but Suzi is afraid and doesn't want to go. When she sees Grandma, Suzi asks Grandpa if she can touch her and notices she looks different, even though she is in her favorite dress. Before leaving for the funeral, Suzi goes to Grandma's room and cries as she realizes she will never see her again. She doesn't want to leave Grandma alone at the cemetery, but she returns to church (for what seems to Suzi) like a big party with lots of food. When everyone prepares to return home, they are comforted because Grandpa is eating and talks about making plans with his friends.

Making Connections

The rituals of death, while comforting to adults, seem awkward and confusing to children. Explaining why certain things happen and involving children when appropriate will help them feel more a part of what is happening around them.

Discussion Questions

- What special memories do you have of someone you know who died?
- How did you and others remember that person after he or she died?
- How did it make you feel to talk about that person when he or she was not there?

Saying Goodbye to Daddy

Vigna, Judith. 1991. *Saying Goodbye to Daddy.*
Morton Grove, Ill.: Albert Whitman.

Story Summary

When Clare's father is killed in a car accident, her mother and grand-father try to help her through the grieving process. She tries to understand what it means to die, but she can only relate to the death of her hamster when her parents told her that it couldn't see, feel cold, or be hungry anymore. Her mother explains how her father will be buried and what the funeral will be like, and she tries to assure Clare that she was not responsible for her father's death because she yelled when she was mad at him. Clare is angry that her father has died and worried that her mother and grandfather will die soon, but they explain that they both expect to live long lives. At the funeral the minister says nice things about Daddy, and at the cemetery Clare and her mother put flowers on the casket after it is lowered into the ground. When they are ready, Clare and her mother go through Daddy's wallet and look at all the special things he saved—including pictures of Clare and a clipping from her time in the school play. She remembers how much her daddy loved her, and even though she still feels sad from time to time, Clare realizes she will always have happy memories of her father.

Making Connections

Children who experience the death of a parent experience a range of emotions that can include fear, sadness, confusion, and anger. Encouraging them to discuss their feelings and share them with others will help children feel less alone in their grief.

Discussion Questions

- How does it make you feel knowing that your parent has died?
- What are some happy thoughts you have of your parent?
- What can you do to make sure you remember all the happy times?

Grandfather's Laika

Wahl, Mats. 1990. *Grandfather's Laika.*
Illustrated by Tord Nygren. Minneapolis, Minn.: Carolrhoda.

Story Summary

Every day Matthew and his grandfather walk home from school with Grandpa's dog Laika. They take notice of the beauty around them and play together in the woods. At home they rest, with Laika lying on his rug and Matthew napping on Laika. Grandpa always says he's going to throw out that old rug, but he never does—Matthew knows it because the rug is special to Laika. One windy and rainy day Grandpa tells him that Laika is sick, but Matthew doesn't want to notice that she is slower and doesn't eat and drink enough anymore. When Grandpa tells him Laika has to be put to sleep, he tries to explain to Matthew that everything that lives must sometime die. Matthew says good-bye to Laika on the day she will be put to sleep, and they bury her deep in the woods near the lake where they used to play. After they bury her, Matthew takes the rug home to remind him of Laika.

Making Connections

One of the fears that children face with the death of a loved one is the fear that they will somehow forget that loved one. Sharing memories and keepsakes will help children understand how people and pets can remain alive in our hearts even after they are gone.

Discussion Questions

- What special memories do you have of someone who has died?
- Do you have a special memento that reminds you of that person?

The Old Dog

Zolotow, Charlotte. 1995. *The Old Dog.*
Illustrated by James Ransome. New York: HarperCollins.

Story Summary

When Ben went to pat his old dog hello one morning, he discovered she no longer wagged her tail. Ben's father confirmed that the old dog had died. When Ben came home from school he drank his milk and played, conscious of the absence of his dog. He thought about death and its meaning, grieving over the loneliness of missing his dog. Through his tears, however, he sees his father arrive with a new puppy.

Making Connections

The loss of a pet may be a child's first experience with death. This book's simple style moves quickly from the loss to getting a new pet. But it recognizes that even with the new pet, the old dog is still missed.

Discussion Questions

- Have you had a pet die?
- What things reminded you of your pet?
- Did you get a new pet right away, or did you wait a while?
- Can a new puppy fully replace a beloved old dog?
- How can you keep memories of your former pet alive?

Who Is Ben?

Zolotow, Charlotte. 1997. *Who Is Ben?*
Illustrated by Kathryn Jacobi. New York: HarperCollins.

Story Summary

Young Ben peers out the front windows of his house on a moonless, starless night, wondering about the darkness. Making his way upstairs, he looks at his bedroom window, unable to see the house across the street, the front steps of his own house, or the tree in his yard. He feels as though he can touch a part of the blackness that was inside and outside, a smooth and velvety blackness that makes him feel safe. When his mother breaks the blackness and turns on a light as she comes in, his room looks like it never has before. Wondering about the process of life, he asks where he was before he was born, and where he will be when he dies, feeling the answer without hearing it from his mother. He finds comfort in the blackness and feels a part of it.

Making Connections

Young children ask questions about and try to understand death for a variety of reasons, often exploring unknown issues with little fear. This story, though not directly dealing with death, helps children relate to the questions and new feelings explored by a young boy.

Discussion Questions

- How do you feel when you are in the dark? Does it make you think of anything?

- Are you afraid of the dark? What is it you are afraid of?

- What do you think happens to people when they die?

CHAPTER 5

Disabilities and Differences

Going with the Flow
by Claire H. Blatchford

Mandy *by Barbara D. Booth*

Arnie and the New Kid
by Nancy L. Carlson

With the Wind *by Liz Damrell*

Be Good to Eddie Lee
by Virginia Fleming

Baby Duck and the Bad Eyeglasses
by Amy Hest

Imagine Me on a Sit-Ski!
by George Moran

Where's Chimpy? *by Berniece Rabe*

The Secret Code
by Dana Meachen Rau

Alex is My Friend
by Marisabina Russo

Just Kids
Visiting a Class for Children with Special Needs
by Ellen B. Senisi

My Brother Matthew *by Mary Thompson*

Going with the Flow

Blatchford, Claire H. 1998. *Going with the Flow*.
Illustrated by Janice Lee Porter. Minneapolis, Minn.: Carolrhoda.

Story Summary

When Mark and his family move to a new city, he faces the frustration of starting a new school with strange new students and teachers—all of whom, he is convinced, stare at only his behind-the-ear hearing aids. Unwilling to face their questions and stares, he spends his first day of school alone in the gym, inconsolable by the interpreter provided for him. A "deal" with his father convinces him to return to school, and Mark slowly begins to accept his new home and school. Making new friends is hard at first, and Mark finds he has to endure the laughter and misunderstandings of the other students. But when he begins to realize that he has many of the abilities that the other kids have, especially as a basketball player, he becomes more comfortable being around them. More importantly, he learns how to become a member of a team, working together for a common goal, and develops friendships that help him understand his capabilities.

Making Connections

For a child who is deaf, starting at a new school and moving to a new home can bring more frustration and confusion than for children facing these challenges without disabilities. Mark's story not only describes how he learned to overcome his fears and make new friends, but is told through a first-person account that provides a unique glimpse of what it is like to live in the world of the deaf.

Discussion Questions

- Why do you think people would stare at Mark's hearing aids?
- Do you know someone who wears hearing aids—or has another disability?
- What kinds of things do you think you could do to help that person feel more comfortable or welcome at school?
- How would you want people to treat you if you had a disability?

Mandy

Booth, Barbara D. 1991. *Mandy.*
Illustrated by Jim LaMarche. New York: Lothrop, Lee & Shepard.

Story Summary

Mandy and her grandmother share a special relationship on the farm in the country. Profoundly deaf and unable to hear, Mandy experiences many joys of the world through the kindness and love of her grandmother. This story not only reflects the strong bond between the two but also, told from Mandy's point of view, presents thoughtful detail on the life of a child who is deaf. Through her grandma, Mandy experiences dancing to music as Grandma places a radio on the floor and dances with Mandy in their shoeless feet. They explore the out-of-doors together, Grandma explaining to Mandy the sounds made by leaves and branches and pointing out the flight of the geese. When Grandma loses a precious pin given to her by Grandpa, it is Mandy's turn to give back to Grandma as she faces the dark of night and an impending storm to search for the pin in the woods. When she at last finds it and presents it to Grandma, their love grows even deeper.

Making Connections

Beyond the story of a child with a disability is the story of the strong sense of connection and the love between a child and her grandmother. Through this story children will understand that having a disability does not impede the development of loving and supportive relationships.

Discussion Questions

- Do you know someone who is deaf? How do you communicate with that person?
- Do you feel differently about that person than about other people because of the deafness?
- What kinds of things can people who are deaf do?

Arnie and the New Kid

Carlson, Nancy L. 1990. *Arnie and the New Kid.*
New York: Viking.

Story Summary

Philip is a new kid at school who is different from most of the other kids—he uses a wheelchair to get around and sometimes needs extra help. He doesn't have many friends because the other children don't know how to play with a boy in a wheelchair. Arnie teases Philip, challenging him to races and commenting on how slowly he eats. When Arnie falls down some stairs, he is taken to the hospital and treated for a broken leg and a broken wrist. He, too, needs help getting around and needs his friends to carry his books for him. Realizing Arnie needs a friend, Philip invites him over to his house where they are able to enjoy many different activities together. After Arnie has his cast removed, he begins to include Philip in his games and activities, including making Philip the coach during their baseball game!

Making Connections

It's difficult for many children to understand the different adjustments made by someone using a wheelchair, especially another child. Reading the story of a child who is temporarily disabled, and comes to better understand someone who is permanently disabled, will provide a unique perspective.

Discussion Questions

- Do you know someone who has a disability? How does it affect what they can and cannot do?

- What kinds of games can you play with someone who has a disability?

With the Wind

Damrell, Liz. 1991. *With the Wind.*
Illustrated by Stephen Marchesi. New York: Orchard.

Story Summary

The simple text of this story is enhanced with full-page illustrations show-ing remarkable perspectives of a young boy riding a horse. The boy, who uses a wheelchair, goes to nearby fields to watch the horses run, and carefully touches his hands to their faces. He is given the opportunity to ride and feels the strength of the horse beneath him, closing his eyes for a time while he rides. As if expe-riencing the dreams of the horse while he rides, the boy seems to sense the horse feeling the earth move away as they ride with other horses, with other people, and as they ride alone. The boy's parents wait for him to return as he savors the strength and sense of freedom, a strength and freedom he only feels while riding the horse because he uses a wheelchair.

Making Connections

Children who use wheelchairs seek opportunities to experience life as it is lived by those who do not use wheelchairs. Knowing how children who use wheelchairs feel can help others better understand how to interact with and support those children.

Discussion Questions

- Do you know anyone who uses a wheelchair? What are some of the things they can't do because they use a wheelchair?

- What are some of the things they can do?

- In what ways are people who use wheelchairs like people who do not use wheelchairs?

Be Good to Eddie Lee

Fleming, Virginia. 1993. *Be Good to Eddie Lee.*
Illustrated by Floyd Cooper. New York: Philomel Books.

Story Summary

Eddie Lee, a child with Down syndrome, tries to join Christy and JimBud as they play. Christy knows she should be kind to him, but JimBud has little patience for him. Christy and JimBud explore the nearby woods, but every time they think they have escaped Eddie Lee, he appears. Christy wants to take a waterlilly home, but it is too far out in the water. Eddie Lee takes her to another pond, where they see frogeyes and more waterlillies. Eddie Lee convinces Christy to leave them in the pond. As they gaze in the pond, Christy's face becomes distorted in the ripples, and Eddie Lee points out that her face now looks funny, but that it's her heart that counts.

Making Connections

Christy and JimBud show different viewpoints on how children struggle when confronted with a mentally disabled child. Although Eddie Lee is indeed mentally disabled, the story shows that he understands important concepts and that he can contribute to their play.

Discussion Questions

- Do you know someone like Eddie Lee? What makes him or her seem different?

- Christy's mama tells her to be good to Eddie Lee. What kinds of things could she do to be good to him?

- How do you think Eddie Lee feels about being left out? How do you feel when you are left out?

- What did Eddie Lee teach Christy?

Baby Duck and the Bad Eyeglasses

Hest, Amy. 1996. *Baby Duck and the Bad Eyeglasses.*
Illustrated by Jill Barton. Cambridge, Mass.: Candlewick.

Story Summary

Baby Duck did not appreciate her new eyeglasses. She just didn't look like herself! She didn't dance, hop, or play for fear her glasses would fall off. When Grampa pointed out that the glasses were red like his, she began to experiment, discovering that they didn't fall off. When Grampa shows her a boat named "Baby," she realizes that being able to read her name with her new glasses is cause for celebration.

Making Connections

Being different can be unsettling. Adjusting to items such as new glasses, a hearing aid, or braces takes time. Adults and peers can help others accept their differences by recognizing the benefits that such aids can bring.

Discussion Questions

- Put your hands over your ears while I talk to you about this book. How does it feel to not be able to hear very well?

- Would you get tired if you had a hard time hearing?

- Would you want something that would help?

- How many people do you know who wear glasses at least part of the time?

- People who can't see well sometimes don't realize they need glasses. Though they want to see, they may worry about being teased. What can you do to help someone who has new glasses or some other type of special aid?

Imagine Me on a Sit-Ski!

Moran, George. 1995. *Imagine Me on a Sit-Ski!*
Illustrated by Nadine Bernard Westcott. Morton Grove, Ill.: Albert Whitman.

Story Summary

Told from the perspective of a young boy named Billy, this story follows a group of children as they learn to ski. Each child has a different disability and faces the challenge of learning to ski with the same sense of nervousness faced by all new skiers. As the children prepare for their first lesson, each one is outfitted with unique adaptive devices that will allow them to enjoy skiing. Some use a walker with small skis on the bottom, while others use crutches with tiny skis on them. Billy and his friend Tommy each use a sit-ski and are carefully guided by ski instructors. The exhilaration of learning to ski for the very first time and the keen sense of awareness of their surroundings the children experience provide many opportunities for children to consider their own first time of learning something new and challenging. The fact that Billy accomplished something as difficult as skiing leads him to consider that there are many other things in the world for him to try, even if he does have a disability.

Making Connections

Learning how to accomplish something as challenging as skiing can be difficult whether or not one has a disability. Reading about Billy and his friends will help children understand that those who have a disability can still participate in many activities.

Discussion Questions

- Can you think of something that you were nervous about doing before you learned how to do it?
- How did you overcome your fear and learn something new?
- What are some other things Billy could learn to do?

Where's Chimpy?

Rabe, Berniece. 1988. *Where's Chimpy?*
Photographs by Diane Schmidt. Niles, Ill.: Albert Whitman.

Story Summary

The beauty of a little girl with Down syndrome is vibrantly depicted in this story illustrated with photographs. Misty has lost her toy Monkey, Chimpy, and doesn't want to go to bed without him. Misty and her Dad retrace the activities of her day, including playing on the swing set with friends, playing with her cat, and playing with her basket of blocks, all in the hopes of finding Chimpy. Learning about the things Misty does in her day also helps children understand how they are similar to Misty. When she does finally find Chimpy, Misty is ready for a bedtime story and ready for sleep—just like other children.

Making Connections

The frustrations of not being able to hold a special pet is understood by many children, and those who read this story will realize that children with disabilities such as Down syndrome have many of the same feelings as those who do not have disabilities.

Discussion Questions

- Do you have a favorite doll or toy you like to keep with you all the time?

- How would feel if you lost it?

- How is Misty different from other children? How is she similar to other children?

The Secret Code

Rau, Dana Meachen. 1998. *The Secret Code.*
Illustrated by Bari Weissman. New York: Children's Press.

Story Summary

Oscar is a young boy who reads with what his friends describe as a "secret code": because he is blind, he uses books that are printed in Braille. When his friends at school notice his books are different, he explains what Braille is and how each set of raised bumps represents a letter. Oscar also teaches his friends how to read Braille, and together they share their joy of reading. In this simply illustrated book that includes a complete chart of the Braille alphabet, children will learn how people with disabilities use special tools to lead fulfilling lives.

Making Connections

Very young children, when faced with a new situation, most often have questions and curiosities about that which is unknown. A story such as *The Secret Code* will give them a chance to better understand children who are blind and, just as important, understand how much they share in common with those who have disabilities.

Discussion Questions

- What kinds of disabilities do your friends or family members have?
- What types of special tools do they use because of their disabilities?
- How do you think you would feel if you couldn't see?

Alex is My Friend

Russo, Marisabina. 1992. *Alex is My Friend*.
New York: Greenwillow.

Story Summary

Growing up with a friend with a disability provides many opportunities for two young boys to grapple with the confusions of life. Alex, who is a dwarf, and his friend met a long time ago when both were little and attended the soccer games of their bigger sisters. They became good friends over the years, playing games and telling silly stories. They shared many things together and always attended each other's birthday parties. As they grew, one boy noticed that Alex, who is older, was smaller than he was. His mother explained that Alex would always be small, but that his mind would continue to grow and learn. Alex eventually has to have an operation on his back and spend a few months in bed recovering. Visiting Alex was at first scary because of his brace, but after sharing a joke the two boys laugh together again. When he returns to school Alex uses a wheelchair to get around the halls, but he is unable to run around with the other children. The two boys find plenty of other things to do, and soon Alex is back on his feet, playing again. Though Alex may be little, it doesn't matter—he is still a good friend.

Making Connections

Told in the first person from the perspective of Alex's friend, this story will help children understand that people with physical disabilities may be very much like those who do not have a disability.

Discussion Questions

- Do you know anyone who has a disability? What kinds of things do you like to do with that person?

- How are you like people who have disabilities?

- How can you help people with disabilities?

Just Kids
Visiting a Class for Children with Special Needs

Senisi, Ellen B. 1998.
Just Kids: Visiting a Class for Children with Special Needs.
New York: Dutton Children's Books.

Story Summary

When Cindy teases a student with special needs, her teacher sends her to the principal's office. He tells her that she is going to spend some time in the classroom for children with special needs so that she can learn about them. The teacher explains to Cindy about the children, and at first Cindy is very uncomfortable with spending time there. But Cindy begins to learn about their conditions, such as epilepsy, autism, emotional and behavioral disorders, Down syndrome, and learning disabilities. Cindy gradually comes to develop an understanding of their differences, and she begins to earn the students' acceptance.

Making Connections

This is a long story that may need to be used in shorter sessions. The photographs provide a realistic setting, making it an especially informative book. Children may feel discomfort when around children from special classes, and reading this book will educate them about their differences.

Discussion Questions

- Do you ever think about how you learned to talk, run, use a scissors, play games, read, or tie your shoes? Was it easy or hard?

- Have you ever seen someone doing something new and wished you could do that too? Perhaps you wanted to learn how to fly a kite or bowl and it was difficult at first. How did you feel if you had trouble learning?

- Did someone help you? Were they kind or did they tease you?

- What kinds of things did Cindy learn about the students? What did you learn that was new?

- What would you still like to learn about students with handicapping conditions?

My Brother Matthew

Thompson, Mary. 1992. *My Brother Matthew.*
New York: Woodbine House.

Story Summary

David's brother Matthew likes cats, something David's family learned during one of their long walks through the neighborhood. He especially likes calico cats, but it took a while for people to understand that because Matthew speaks differently than other people. He also moves and behaves differently because he was born with disabilities. When Matthew was born, David was too young to understand what was going on—only that Grandma stayed with him, and Mom and Dad were at the hospital a lot. The first time David saw Matthew he was very small and had a lot of tubes to help him breathe and eat. It took a long time for Matthew to come home, time during which David's mom and dad spent many days and nights at the hospital, even missing David's birthday. When Matthew finally came home, David had a hard time adjusting to all the special attention his parents had to pay Matthew. As he grew and got a little stronger David began to do things his brother smiled at and seemed to enjoy—much to the surprise and delight of his parents. They played a lot of games together and had a special bond that includes David being the only one in the family who could always understand what Matthew said and wanted. Though there are times David gets tired of his little brother always following and copying him, and occasionally embarrassing him, things like that don't matter when Matthew achieves new things like walking. David hopes Matthew can eventually learn to ride a bike and visit even more cats than he can while walking.

Making Connections

Having a sibling with disabilities can be difficult for children to understand and explain to others. Talking openly about the disability and answering questions can begin to lead to better understanding.

Discussion Questions

- Do you know someone with a disability? How does it make you feel?
- What kinds of disabilities can people have that other people can't see?

CHAPTER 6

Families

My Family
by Debbie Bailey

Twinnies
by Eve Bunting

Twins
by Monica Colli

My Mother's Getting Married
by Joan Drescher

Boundless Grace
by Mary Hoffman

Zelda and Ivy
by Laura McGee Kvasnosky

One Up, One Down
by Carol Snyder

My Two Uncles
by Judith Vigna

Daddy's Roommate
by Michael Willhoite

My Family

Bailey, Debbie. 1998. *My Family.*
Photographs by Susan Huszar. Willowdale, Ontario: Annick.

Story Summary

A book of bright photos and simple text for very young children, *My Family* depicts different kinds of families in natural settings and familiar situations. Children will see how families take care of each other, love one another, share special celebrations and enjoy being together. They'll also understand that this love exists in families of different sizes and ethnic backgrounds, and they'll see situations that remind them of their family.

Making Connections

Understanding the security and love that exists within families, no matter their size or cultural background, will help young children develop confidence in themselves and their abilities.

Discussion Questions

- Who are the people in your family? Do you have some friends with different families?

- In what ways are they different? In what ways are they the same?

- What are the ways in which you and your family show each other love and support?

Twinnies

Bunting, Eve. 1997. *Twinnies.*
Illustrated by Nancy Carpenter. San Diego, Calif.: Harcourt Brace.

Story Summary

The arrival of twins means the big sister not only has to make room for two siblings, she has to learn to deal with new situations and new ways of living. There's also a lot of new stuff in the house—two cribs, two high chairs, two strollers, two sets of clothes—things that leave little room for playing games. The twins seem take up a lot of room outside, too, crowding big sister out on the sidewalk and attracting the attention of other people. "Somebody's jealous," says one lady, noticing the reaction big sister has to the attention heaped onto the twins. "My name's not 'somebody'," sister replies, asserting herself as an individual. She eventually learns how she can help out around the house and care for the twins, but she finds she is no longer the center of attention like she used to be before the twins arrived. She used to be the special one, and though her father emphasizes his love for her, she finds it hard to feel special with all the attention the twins get. She eventually learns how much she loves them, however, and how much she enjoys being their big sister.

Making Connections

Welcoming a new baby can be an exciting yet intimidating experience for any child. Welcoming twins means double the excitement—and can mean double the intimidation. This story helps children understand and acknowledge the confusing feelings they may have around living with twins.

Discussion Questions

- How did you feel when you found out you were going to have more than one brother or sister?

- Do you know other people who have twins at home? Do they seem to act differently than people who do not have twins?

- What makes you unique from the twins? How is each twin different from the other one?

Twins

Colli, Monica. 1992. *Twins.*
Illustrated by Filippo Brunello. New York: Child's Play (Ltd.).

Story Summary

Having lived with being compared to her twin sister all her young life, a little girl does her best to distinguish herself from her twin. Simple text leads the reader through many examples of how the two girls, though they look identical, are very different from one another in personality and behavior. The story is told from the perspective of one of the twins, who begins by saying her sister is the "nasty one," and the one who is messy, fibs, and is not as strong as she. Though she repeatedly tries to find and draw attention to the things that make her different from her twin, she comes to understand that being a twin isn't so bad after all, and that in her twin sister she has a special, lifelong friend.

Making Connections

From the perspective of one twin, this story will give twin children a chance to understand how they are each individual in their own right, but also part of a special relationship shared by few.

Discussion Questions

- How are you and your twin different from each other? How are you alike?

- What do you think life would be like if you were not a twin?

- What do you like about having a twin?

My Mother's Getting Married

Drescher, Joan. 1986. *My Mother's Getting Married.*
New York: Dial Books for Young Readers.

Story Summary

Katy's mother is getting married, and everybody but Katy thinks it is wonderful. She worries she and her mom won't get to have special times alone anymore—like picnics at the beach, staying up late and watching movies, and having fun. Katy worries her mom's new husband Ben will eat all her cereal and that mom will only go out with him anymore. Katy invites her classmates to the wedding and makes special invitations but is still not excited. She is a flower girl and gets to wear a beautiful dress for the wedding, but she still wishes they weren't getting married. On the day of the wedding she sees how happy her mom is and realizes she is happy too. They get to eat a good cake and Katy catches the bouquet. When Katy shares her feelings with her Mom and tells her she doesn't want them to go on their honeymoon, Mom promises Katy they will always have special times together, and that she'll always be her Katydid.

Making Connections

When children are faced with a parent remarrying they may naturally feel fearful about their new situation. Explaining the special relationship that children will have with both parents may help reduce the anxiety.

Discussion Questions

- What are your favorite things to do with your mom or dad?

- What activities will you share with your stepparent and stepsiblings?

- What are some special things you and your mom or dad can still share, even though you'll have a new family?

Boundless Grace

Hoffman, Mary. 1995. *Boundless Grace*.
Illustrated by Caroline Binch. New York: Dial Books for Young Readers.

Story Summary

Grace lives with her mother and grandmother. She isn't interested in the fact that her father lives in Africa, but she wishes she had a perfect family that included a father, brother, and dog. Her father sends tickets for her and her grandmother to visit him in Africa, where she confronts her stepfamily. Grace feels discontented, becoming cross with her stepmother, just like she has read about in the fairy tales. Gradually she becomes accustomed to her new family, realizing that it's fine that some families don't fit the fairy tale model.

Making Connections

Many traditional stories feature stereotypes, such as the wicked stepmother in fairy tales or families with two children and two parents. Grace confronts an alternative family *and* an exotic setting. Through support from her caring extended family she realizes that differences can be enriching.

Discussion Questions?

- Do you have family members who live in different places?
- Do you have many different kinds of family, such as stepparents, half-siblings, or adopted siblings?
- What problems can you face with unusual families?
- What good things happen when you have extra grandparents or other relatives?

Zelda and Ivy

Kvasnosky, Laura McGee. 1998. *Zelda and Ivy.*
Cambridge, Mass.: Candlewick.

Story Summary

Zelda and Ivy are sisters, playing together and sharing adventures. Because Zelda is the oldest, she often makes the decisions about what they will play, who will go first, and what Ivy will do as they play. Her instructions often lead Ivy to do things that cause her to get hurt or might get her into trouble, but Ivy does them anyway because Zelda is the oldest. Whether it's playing on the swing, making themselves look pretty, or dreaming of magic, the two sisters share a strong bond of love and affection.

Making Connections

As children grow, they often find themselves at odds with their sisters and brothers because of the differences in their ages and developmental stages. Understanding that these changes will occur, but that they will always be family, will help children adjust to the changes in their relationships with their siblings.

Discussion Questions

- What kinds of feelings do you have for your brother or sister?
- Are there things you used to do together that you don't enjoy anymore?
- What kinds of things do you still like to do and share with your brother or sister?

One Up, One Down

Snyder, Carol. 1994. *One Up, One Down.*
Illustrated by Maxie Chambliss. New York: Atheneum.

Story Summary

For Katie, life as the older sister to twins can be trying and exhausting, especially when the twins always seem to need things at different times. Katie looks in the mirror and sees that she hasn't changed, but her world certainly has with the arrival of nonidentical twins. They're dissimilar in other ways too. They act differently: one wants to be held up while the other wants to be down on the ground, one is wet while the other is dry, one wants to sleep while the other is awake—differences that often lead to exhausting yet amusing situations. Katie knows she is a good big sister though, helping out at mealtimes, playing with the twins, and helping to accommodate what seems to be their constant need for one to be up, and one to be down. Though she's tired all the time, she finds joy in helping her sisters learn—especially when their first words are "one up, one down!"

Making Connections

Recognizing the dramatic changes that take place when new siblings come home, especially twins, is important for parents helping older children adjust. This story provides light humor for older children learning to cope with the arrival of twins.

Discussion Questions

- How is life different for you and your family now that there are twins in the house?

- Do you remember how things were before the twins arrived? Are there things you used to do that you would like to be able to do again?

- What have you learned about being an older sister or brother?

- What are your special responsibilities in caring for the twins?

My Two Uncles

Vigna, Judith. 1995. *My Two Uncles*.
Morton Grove, Ill.: Albert Whitman.

Story Summary

Elly's Uncle Ned has a special friend she calls Uncle Phil. They live in an apartment together that Elly loves to visit. She and her uncles paint and make things when she comes to visit, and they have many adventures together. On one visit they decide to make a special gift for her grandparents, who are going to celebrate their 50th wedding anniversary at a special party. The entire family is invited, except that Uncle Ned is told he cannot bring Uncle Phil. Elly is confused when she sees how harshly her grandfather reacts to the idea that both her uncles may attend. She asks her daddy why Grandfather doesn't like them, and he explains that it's because they are gay. Wishing her grandfather could accept her uncles, she watches from afar on the day of the party when Uncle Ned brings the present they had made together. Elly feels the party isn't as much fun as it would be with both her uncles, and her grandfather acknowledges that perhaps he is being too stubborn. The next day, when they all go to visit the uncles after church, Elly's grandfather waves to them from the car—the first time he has ever acknowledged them.

Making Connections

When children first learn about homosexuality they develop feelings based in part on how the adults around them react. Explaining homosexuality and being honest about it will help children better understand when others may be different.

Discussion Questions

- Do you understand what it means to be gay?
- In what ways do people show their love for one another?
- How can you show your love for someone who is gay?

Daddy's Roommate

Willhoite, Michael. 1990. *Daddy's Roommate.*
Boston, Mass.: Alyson Wonderland.

Story Summary

A young boy talks about his life after his mom and dad get a divorce and his dad gets a new roommate named Frank. Dad and Frank do everything together—work, eat, sleep, shave, and even fight. Frank likes the boy, and he does lots of things with him too—they catch bugs, read, and make lunches together. On the weekends when the boy visits his dad and Frank they do a lot of fun things together—go to ball games and the zoo, work in the yard, go to the beach. When Mommy tells the boy his dad and Frank are gay, he doesn't understand and needs Mommy to explain that it is just one more kind of love. Daddy and his roommate are very happy together, and that makes the boy happy too.

Making Connections

Homosexuality, while at first difficult, can be understood when children accept it as love between two people.

Discussion Questions

- Do you know someone who is homosexual?
- How do they show their love for one another?
- How do they show their love for you?

CHAPTER 7

Fears

Left Behind
by Carol Carrick

Daisy Dare
by Anita Jeram

The Night the Scary Beasties Popped Out of My Head
by Daniel Kamish and David Kamish

Thundercake
by Patricia Polacco

Whitewash
by Ntozake Shange

Darkness
by Mildred Pitts Walter

Left Behind

Carrick, Carol. 1988. *Left Behind.*
Illustrated by Donald Carrick. New York: Clarion.

Story Summary

When Christopher's class goes on a field trip to the aquarium everyone works hard to stay with their partner, even on the crowded subway train. On the way back Christopher gets separated from his class and realizes, when he gets pushed off the train, that he can't get back on. He doesn't know what to do so waits where he is and hopes somebody will be able to help him. A subway attendant sees him and takes him to the police who are able track down his teacher. Christopher worries that she will be mad and that the other kids will think he is dumb for getting lost from the group, but everyone is just glad he is all right and glad to see him again.

Making Connections

When children become lost or separated from a group, their emotions can range from fear and sadness to worrying about possible consequences when they are reunited. Understanding what to do in case they do become lost will help children deal with the situation when they are confronted with it.

Discussion Questions

- Do you ever remember being lost? How did it make you feel?
- Do you know what to do in case you get lost?

Daisy Dare

Jeram, Anita. 1995. *Daisy Dare.*
Cambridge, Mass.: Candlewick.

Story Summary

Daisy Dare, an invincible young mouse, insists that she is never scared. Her friends dare her to do a variety of things, such as eating a worm. She accepts each dare with glee. But then one day they dare her to steal the bell off the collar of the sleeping cat. She barely escapes! As she and her friends celebrate, she declares that she is only *sometimes* scared.

Making Connections

Creating dares can be deliciously fun as long as no one is truly in danger. This celebration of conquering fear also shows that accepting a dare can be risky.

Discussion Questions

- Have you ever accepted a dare?
- Were you sorry that you accepted it?
- Would a good friend dare you to do something truly dangerous?
- When should you *not* accept a dare?
- Can you think of some dares that would be fun without being scary?

The Night the Scary Beasties Popped Out of My Head

Kamish, Daniel, and David Kamish. 1998.
The Night the Scary Beasties Popped Out of My Head.
New York: Random House.

Story Summary

Dan's sleep is suddenly disrupted by variety of noises. He grabs a pencil and draws the nightmare Beastie, thinking that if he erases it the noises will stop. But the Beastie comes alive. Then the Boogie joins the Beastie, and Dan has to become creative to stop the chaos. He draws a special dog and a fire engine to chase the monsters. Finally he sends them away through the showers and erases them out of the night. He no longer fears the nightmares, but he keeps his pencil close, just in case.

Making Connections

Bad dreams can be terrifying at any age. Be sure to note how a father-and-son team created this book. The childlike illustrations and perspective offer students ample opportunities to explore the challenges of nightmares in a nonthreatening context.

Discussion Questions

- What are your good dreams about?
- What are your nightmares about?
- How did Dan handle his nightmares?
- What do you do when you have bad dreams?
- Dan erased his nightmares and then showered them away. What other things can you do if you get scared at night?

Thundercake

Polacco, Patricia. 1990. *Thundercake*.
New York: Philomel.

Story Summary

This beautiful, folk-art illustrated book is the story of a grandmother who helps her granddaughter deal with her fear of thunder. During the summer there are frequent thunderstorms that often compel Grandmother to bake a thundercake. With each clap of thunder the grandmother and her granddaughter count the seconds between the bolt of lightning and the sound of thunder, thus figuring out how far away the storm is and how long they have to get all the ingredients together for the thundercake. First the eggs, then the chocolate, sugar and flour, then tomatoes and strawberries are all gathered while they count the distance of the approaching storm. The cake finally goes into the oven just before the storm arrives. The granddaughter listens to her grandmother tell her how brave she is for getting all the ingredients from the different and scary parts of the farm and how she has overcome her fear of the thunder. As the storm reaches them the cake is ready to come out of the oven and they quietly watch the storm pass overhead.

Making Connections

Fears of the dark, of loud noises, or of thunderstorms are common among young children. Helping them overcome their fears by talking about their feelings and gently confronting them will lead to an ability to face their fears in the future.

Discussion Questions

- What are the things that frighten you? Do you know why you are afraid?
- What are some things you can do to keep yourself from feeling afraid?
- What are some happy things you can think about when your are afraid?

Whitewash

Shange, Ntozake. 1977. *Whitewash*.
Illustrated by Michael Sporn. New York: Walker.

Story Summary

Helene-Angel's day starts to disintegrate when she gets called on in class when she isn't paying attention. After school, she waits for her brother, Mauricio, to walk her home. On their way, a gang of boys corners them, calling them "mud people." The gang beats Mauricio and paints Helene-Angel's face white. Mauricio carries her home, where her grandmother cleans her up. Even after the paint is gone, Helene-Angel sees it on her face, and she refuses to leave her room. After a week, her grandmother insists that she must be strong. She comes out of her room to find a group of friends who pledge to stay with her so that she'll not be taunted again.

Making Connections

Being exposed to racism can be traumatizing at any age. Helene-Angel's grandmother honors her self-protective response, but she encourages her to face her fears with the help of her friends. This book shows the importance of support systems when facing threatening situations.

Discussion Questions

- Has anyone ever teased you because you are different? How did it make you feel?
- What would you want to do if this happened to you?
- Who would you turn to for support if this happened to you?
- How could you help a friend who has been hurt by someone else?

Darkness

Walter, Mildred Pitts. 1995. *Darkness.*
Illustrated by Marcia Jameson. New York: Simon & Schuster.

Story Summary

Of all the childhood maladies, being afraid of the dark is one of the most universal. In this beautifully illustrated story readers are encouraged to think of all the wonderful things that happen in the dark. Falling stars can only be seen in the dark, life begins in the dark, seeds take root in the darkness of the earth, precious gems are formed in the dark reaches of the earth, dark clouds bring refreshing rain, and our friend the shadow is dark. When night falls, and friends and family gather together, the sky turns dark. Wonderful dreams happen in the dark, too, right before daybreak.

Making Connections

Confronting fears, such as being afraid of the dark, can provide opportunities for children to begin to understand and overcome their fears.

Discussion Questions

- What makes you afraid? What is it about those things that makes you afraid?
- What happy things can you think of to make you feel less afraid?

CHAPTER 8
Feelings

The Chocolate-Covered-Cookie Tantrum
by Deborah Blumenthal

Anna's Goodbye Apron *by Julie Brillhart*

Used-Up Bear *by Clay Carmichael*

Today I Feel Silly & Other Moods That Make My Day
by Jamie Lee Curtis

The Grumpy Morning
by Pamela Duncan Edwards

Making Room *by Phoebe Koehler*

How Do I Feel About Making Friends
by Sarah Levete

Badger's Bad Mood *by Hiawyn Oram*

Contrary Bear *by Phyllis Root*

Beginning School *by Irene Smalls*

I Miss Franklin P. Shuckles
by Ulana Snihura

Somewhere Today
A Book of Peace
by Shelley Moore Thomas

The Chocolate-Covered-Cookie Tantrum

Blumenthal, Deborah. 1996. *The Chocolate-Covered-Cookie Tantrum.*
Illustrated by Harvey Stevenson. New York: Clarion.

Story Summary

When Sophie sees a girl at the park eating a chocolate-covered cookie she decides she wants one also. Her mother patiently explains that she doesn't have a cookie and that it is almost time for supper. But Sophie insists she wants a chocolate-covered cookie immediately. Her frustration escalates into a full-blown temper tantrum. Finally she is exhausted and they go home. Sophie takes a nap and wakes up to eat all her dinner. Then her mother surprises her with a chocolate-covered cookie for dessert.

Making Connections

Feelings of frustration can escalate when a person is already tired. Sophie's anger is clearly portrayed through the bold and sometimes frantic illustrations. Understanding how to postpone demands until a more appropriate time is an important step toward self-monitoring behavior.

Discussion Questions

- Have you ever wanted something that you couldn't have right away?
- How did you feel about it?
- Do temper tantrums make you feel better or worse?
- What can you do instead of having a tantrum?

Anna's Goodbye Apron

Brillhart, Julie. 1990. *Anna's Goodbye Apron.*
Niles, Ill.: Albert Whitman.

Story Summary

Anna has been a kindergarten teacher at her school for a very long time and is going to move. The children are going to miss her and remember all the wonderful things she did for them like taking them sledding, painting pictures, and making cookies together. They talk about Anna's dog Maggie, who is going to have puppies, and are sad because they won't be able to see the new puppies. On Anna's last day the children give her a special present, an apron on which they had each drawn a special picture and written their names. Anna loves the apron and promises to wear it a lot. A few weeks later Anna sends the kids a letter with some cookies—and tells them she made them with her new friends, Maggie's puppies!

Making Connections

Teachers are the most significant adults in the lives of children besides their parents, and their leaving in the middle of a school year can be very difficult. Talking with children about their experiences and reminding them of the special times will help deal with the sadness they may feel.

Discussion Questions

- What special things have you done with your teacher?
- What makes your teacher such a special person?
- What happy memories will you have of your teacher after she or he leaves?

Used-Up Bear

Carmichael, Clay. 1998. *Used-Up Bear*.
New York: North-South Books.

Story Summary

Bear is Clara's special friend and has been for a long time. So long, in fact, that Bear worries his "worn out" state of dingy white fur, frayed stuffing, loose eye, and drooping nose will make him a "used-up bear" she no longer wants. He considers the possibilities before him, including being used as a dust rag, tossed in the dark cellar, or dropped in the thrift box at a garage sale. Bear tries to make himself invisible so Clara won't notice he's getting worn out, and the other stuffed animals tease him about his age and tell him he'll no longer be Clara's best friend. He awakens one morning, however, to discover that someone has cleaned and repaired him and given him a special new suit—and reminded him how much he is loved, no matter how old he grows.

Making Connections

As children grow and develop new interests, or watch others grow, trying to understand and deal with the emotions of change can be hard. *Used-Up Bear* can help children understand the change that comes with the passage of time and recognize the importance of maintaining special friendships.

Discussion Questions

- Can you think of ways you have changed from when you were smaller?
- What were some of your favorite toys or games to play?
- How have your friends and family changed as they've gotten older?
- How do you think you will change as you continue to grow?

Today I Feel Silly &
Other Moods That Make My Day

Curtis, Jamie Lee. 1998. *Today I Feel Silly & Other Moods That Make My Day.*
Illustrated by Laura Cornell. New York: HarperCollins.

Story Summary

A little girl wakes up feeling silly. She puts rouge on the cat and gloves on her feet. Another day she feels grumpy and mean. One day she's joyful, with a first-rate mood. Each day she discusses her mood and how she feels as she faces varying circumstances. The final page of the book provides a face with turn wheels so that readers can choose their moods.

Making Connections

Understanding that moods change frequently helps a youngster cope. Indeed, just putting a name to a mood can help a person deal with the events that may prompt the emotions.

Discussion Questions

- How do you feel today? Happy? Excited? Sad? Angry?
- Are there reasons why you feel that way?
- Do you sometimes wake up "on the wrong side of the bed" and not know why you feel unhappy?
- Can you ever change how you feel? How?

The Grumpy Morning

Edwards, Pamela Duncan. 1998. *The Grumpy Morning*.
Illustrated by Darcia Labrosse. New York: Hyperion Books for Children.

Story Summary

As morning comes to the farm, the animals share with each other their feelings of frustration at not being cared for. The cow needs to be milked, the dog and goat need to be fed, and the cat needs to be cuddled. None of their needs have been met—and none of them are happy about it. When they go in search of the farmer, they find her in her bed, still asleep. Awakening to the animals on her bed, she realizes they need her and cheerily feeds them, cares for them, and gives them her love.

Making Connections

Growing children experience new emotions and feelings as they learn new things and seek independence. Understanding how to accept their feelings and deal with them will help them better understand what creates those feelings.

Discussion Questions

- Do you sometimes feel bad and don't know why?
- How did you behave when you felt angry or sad?
- What can you do to help yourself feel better?

Making Room

Koehler, Phoebe. 1993. *Making Room.*
New York: Bradbury.

Story Summary

The nice brown dog enjoys the good life with his master—long walks, lazy lunches, and cozy evenings on the couch. His nice life changes when the lady comes along, and his master takes quick walks, goes out to eat, and doesn't make room on the couch anymore. Things get better when the lady scratches his ears and makes special dishes for him to clean up—until the cat comes. The cat hides the dog's toys and makes him share the dishes—but fights well and helps keep the bed warm. All is well until the baby comes, who makes everybody be quiet, takes all the milk, and makes the dog and cat sleep on the rug. As the baby grows, though, things seem to get better—they take long walks again, there are scraps of food on the floor, and the baby makes the dog laugh. He decides to try to make room for everyone.

Making connections

Welcoming a new pet, a new sibling, or a new parent can be a confusing and difficult transition time for everyone, especially young children. Discussing their feelings and explaining the concept of sharing may ease the difficulties they face.

Discussion Questions

- What do you think would change if you had to share your things with someone?
- Can you think of some fun things that you would like to share?

How Do I Feel About Making Friends

Levete, Sarah. 1998. *How Do I Feel About Making Friends.*
Brookfield, Conn.: Copper Beech.

Story Summary

This nonfiction look at friendships features photographs and illustrations of young children learning about and sharing what they know about friendships. Chapters deal with topics such as feeling lonely, making friends, how to work at friendships, and getting through difficult times with friends. Each chapter includes a story about friends, feelings experienced in certain situations, how the children dealt with each situation, and what they learned. Children will appreciate learning from the stories in the book and from the ways in which their own experiences mirror those of the children shown in each chapter.

Making Connections

Making friends and maintaining those friendships can be challenging and rewarding. As children grow and develop new interests, they will also develop new friendships that will lead to new feelings and experiences.

Discussion Questions

- How do you feel about the friends in your life?

- Have you ever been angry with a friend or lonely because you had no friends with whom you could play?

- What kinds of things can you do for your friends when they are feeling lonely or sad?

Badger's Bad Mood

Oram, Hiawyn. 1998. *Badger's Bad Mood*.
Illustrated by Susan Varley. New York: Arthur A. Levine.

Story Summary

When Badger's friends discover that he is in a bad mood, they are surprised that their good friend, who is always happy, would be unhappy. They visit him to try to cheer him, but nothing they can say seems to help. His friend the Mole, as worried as he is, accepts Badger's apologies, who explains he feels he is no good for anything. Other friends are upset because Badger had promised to help them with things, and in his bad mood they fear he will be unable to help. Realizing he may need to feel special and appreciated, his friends arrange a ceremony in which they'll all be recognized for the special things they do—especially Badger, who is so pleased by the support of his friends that he leads a dance in the woods.

Making Connections

Most adults realize that moods and feelings often come and go with no apparent reason, but for young children whose curiosity drives a need to know, unexplained feelings can be very frustrating. Helping children understand their feelings will lead to greater acceptance and an ability to work through them.

Discussion Questions

- Have you ever found yourself in a bad mood and couldn't understand why?

- What have you done for friends and family when you've found they were in a bad mood?

- What do you think you could do the next time you feel sad or angry about something?

Contrary Bear

Root, Phyllis. 1996. *Contrary Bear*.
Illustrated by Laura Cornell. New York: HarperCollins.

Story Summary

A little girl's bear misbehaves regularly. He stomps around the room, throws sand, makes noise, and generally acts contrarily. After the bear gets a thorough soaking in the tub, Dad hangs him up to dry, declaring "No more bear!" That night the little girl promises that the bear has agreed to behave better the next night, and they all share extra hugs and kisses. A similar story is Anita Jeram's *Contrary Mary* (Cambridge, Mass.: Candlewick, 1995).

Making Connections

Placing the blame elsewhere for misbehavior can diffuse tension, even when everyone knows who is really misbehaving. The father shows patience, but he makes it clear when things have gone too far. The bear becomes a useful way to gently confront feelings of frustration often encountered when growing up.

Discussion Questions

- Do you ever misbehave and not know why you've been like that?
- Do you ever blame someone or something else?
- This little girl blames her bear. Does her dad really know who's been contrary?
- What can you do to help when you have contrary feelings?

Beginning School

Smalls, Irene. 1996. *Beginning School.*
Illustrated by Toni Goffe. Parsippany, N.J.: Silver Burdett Press.

Story Summary

Starting school can be an anxious time, and it's no different for Alicia and all her new friends in kindergarten. Everyone says good-bye to their parents and grandparents, sisters and brothers, and aunts and uncles and enters the classroom for their first day. Alicia is amazed by all the wonderful things to see in her classroom, and spends the next days, weeks, and months learning and playing and becoming more comfortable with going to school each day. Her friend Robert takes a little longer to get used to school, but by the time the holiday break arrives in midyear, all the children, while looking forward to the holiday season, are eager for school to begin again after their break.

Making Connections

All children experience different levels of worry and questioning when they begin school, and reading this story helps them understand that their fears and confusion are normal and common.

Discussion Questions

- What do/did you think the first day of school will be/was like?
- What was your favorite thing to do at school?
- Who are some of the new friends you made at school?

I Miss Franklin P. Shuckles

Snihura, Ulana. 1998. *I Miss Franklin P. Shuckles.*
Illustrations by Leanne Franson. Toronto: Annick.

Story Summary

Molly Pepper is friends with Franklin P. Shuckles, the boy who moved next door during the summertime. They play every day, even though Franklin can't throw a ball or play catch very well, and Molly learns to appreciate his funny stories. When school begins, Molly distances herself from Franklin because everyone makes fun of his skinny legs and glasses, and she is afraid that if she remains his friend the other kids will make fun of her, too. She tries to discourage Franklin from being her friend, but nothing she tries works—until she writes him a note saying she doesn't like him anymore. Molly finds herself lonely for her friend when he no longer sits with her or plays with her, and she feels sad when he starts to play with the other boys in the neighborhood. Realizing how much she misses him, Molly lets Franklin know how special he is and is grateful he is willing to forgive her and be her friend again.

Making Connections

Understanding the importance and frailties of friendship can be a difficult lesson for young children, especially when they seek to be accepted by others. Respecting the feelings of others, including those friends who appear to be "different," will lead children to better appreciate each of their friends.

Discussion Questions

- What kinds of friends do you have in your life? How are they alike?
- How are they different from one another? What makes your friends special?

Somewhere Today
A Book of Peace

Thomas, Shelley Moore. 1998. *Somewhere Today: A Book of Peace*. Photographs by Eric Futran. Morton Grove, Ill.: Albert Whitman.

Story Summary

In addition to the friends children know and care about each day, there are many "friends of the world." The photographs presented in *Somewhere Today* are accompanied by simple words that explain how individuals strive to make differences in the lives of others. Whether being a friend, caring for a child or old person, teaching or learning, or planting a tree, children will begin to understand how their own actions can make the world a better place.

Making Connections

Young children's view of the world is relatively small and naturally limited to their own families, neighborhood friends, or school experiences. Sharing the realities of children in other countries and cultures will give children a way to develop a more global perspective and understanding of the world.

Discussion Questions

- In what ways do you and your friends make the world a better place?
- What kinds of things do you think children in other parts of the world like to do with their friends?
- How has one of your friends shown you kindness?

CHAPTER 9

Growing Up

I Did It, I'm Sorry

Buehner, Caralyn. 1998. *I Did It, I'm Sorry.*
Illustrated by Mark Buehner. New York: Dial Books for Young Readers.

Story Summary

Filled with stories of moral dilemmas faced by a variety of animals, *I Did It, I'm Sorry* provides examples in which the reader is presented with the facts of the situation, the opportunity to understand the consequences, and three choices of what could be done. The story provides an added dimension of exploration, as the authors have carefully hidden the corresponding letter of the correct answer in the full-page color illustrations that accompany each story. Though the situations are literally about the animals they depict, such as whether Harlan Monk the Monkey should break the law like his friends and swing from a mava-mava vine, children will be able to relate to key aspects of the stories, like why we have laws. As children grow they learn about many of the values shown in the story, including being dependable, why they shouldn't cheat, the importance of telling the truth, and sharing with friends. Discussing the choices presented with each situation provides wonderful opportunities for children to learn the value of doing what is right.

Making Connections

Teaching values and helping children become more comfortable in a grown-up world is hard to teach through simple words. Sharing this story, through the illustrations and unique situations faced by each animal, will provide adults the context with which to discuss these values with children.

Discussion Questions

- Which stories remind you of situations you have faced?
- How did you decide what was the right thing to do?
- If you were faced with a new situation and didn't know what to do, where could you go for help?

Arnie Goes to Camp

Carlson, Nancy L. 1988. *Arnie Goes to Camp.*
New York: Viking Kestrel.

Story Summary

Leaving home for the first time can be a scary experience for children of any age. When Arnie learns he is going away to summer camp for two weeks he doesn't believe his mother when she says he will love it. On the bus to camp and when he first arrives everyone seems to be very excited and happy, singing songs and playing games—everyone except Arnie. He isn't able to eat lunch and doesn't want to take a nap when it's time. As the days go by he becomes more and more comfortable with the other kids and begins to enjoy all the activities of camp—hiking, sitting around the campfire singing songs and telling stories, playing games, doing arts and crafts, and going canoeing. His postcards home share with his mom how much he enjoys camp. When the time comes to go home, Arnie realizes how much he will miss camp and his new friends—and can't wait to go back the next summer!

Making Connections

Going away to summer camp or having overnight experiences away from family can be frightening and exciting but is important, as children learn to develop a sense of independence. Understanding the emotions one child experiences in this story will help other children prepare for their own experiences.

Discussion Questions

- Have you ever been away from home before? Have you ever been away from home without your parents before?

- What kinds of things do you think you could learn about yourself if you went away without your parents?

- What have you learned that will help you prepare for going away by yourself?

My Own Big Bed

Hines, Anna Grossnickle. 1998. *My Own Big Bed.*
Illustrated by Mary Watson. New York: Greenwillow.

Story Summary

A little girl has a brand-new bed and looks forward to leaving her crib behind—almost. When she worries about falling out, she covers the floor with pillows. She uses stuffed animals to ward off possible loneliness. After dealing with other concerns, she is ready to sleep in her own big bed.

Making Connections

Making transitions such as using a bed instead of a crib can cause discomfort in a youngster. Finding ways to handle potential fears proves to be this young child's strength.

Discussion Questions

- Do you remember the first time you slept in a big bed? Was it scary?
- Can you remember the first time you sat in a booster seat?
- Can you remember other "firsts?" Were they scary or exciting or both?
- How can you help yourself feel more comfortable when doing new things, going new places, or changing to something different?

Little Louie
the Baby Bloomer

Krause, Robert. 1998. *Little Louie the Baby Bloomer.*
Illustrated by Jose Aruego and Ariane Dewey. New York: HarperCollins.

Story Summary

Leo wondered why Little Louie, his younger brother, couldn't throw a ball, pull a wagon, or do other typical little lion activities. His mother reassured him that Louie was normal, but was a late bloomer like Leo once was. Leo tries unsuccessfully to teach Louie but finally gives up. Unexpectedly, Louie catches on—except that he still can't talk.

Making Connections

A child often feels insecure about mastering new skills, especially when an older sibling seems so competent. Although this is told from the point of view of the older sibling, it will prove reassuring to younger siblings who are developing at their own rate.

Discussion Questions

- Do you remember what age you were when you learned to talk, walk, or drink from a cup?

- Did you feel frustrated when you couldn't learn things quickly?

- Do you have a younger brother or sister who you try to teach? Is it hard to teach someone something?

- Do you have an older brother or sister who gets impatient with you when you can't do something right?

- What can you do to feel better when you or others need extra time to learn something new?

How Do I Feel About Looking After Myself

Levete, Sarah. 1998. *How Do I Feel About Looking After Myself.*
Brookfield, Conn.: Copper Beech.

Story Summary

Using a combination of photographs and drawings, *Looking After Myself*
explains in chapter-book format factual information about different things from
being happy and healthy, to having fun, to how to deal with strangers and people
who make children feel uncomfortable. Readers will learn the importance of
keeping teeth and bodies clean and healthy, both inside and out. Chapters about
being "out and about" and "what feels OK" cover such topics as what to do if
you get lost, what to say to strangers who offer rides or candy, and the difference between good touches and bad touches. Each chapter includes a story
about the children in the pictures, information about similar situations, and
how each situation could be handled. A final chapter reminds readers of the
messages presented in the book, and provides points of discussion for children
wanting to talk more about what they have read.

Making Connections

As children grow and learn more about the world, they face new and
often challenging situations. Reading *Looking After Myself* will help them see
other children in similar situations and provide them with a place to begin
understanding.

Discussion Questions

- Which situations described in the book have you faced before?

- How did you handle yourself?

- Are there other things that have happened to you and that you didn't
  know what to do about? In what ways can you keep yourself safe,
  healthy, and happy?

The Last Noo-Noo

Murphy, Jill. 1995. *The Last Noo-Noo.*
Cambridge, Mass.: Candlewick.

Story Summary

Marlon's grandmother thinks he is too old to be using a pacifier. Marlon's mother explains that he only uses his noo-noo, or pacifier, when he is tired, but his grandmother insists it will ruin his monster teeth. Finally, Marlon's mom throws away all his noo-noos, not realizing that he had more hidden in secret places. Eventually the noo-noos nearly all disappear, and Marlon takes his last one and plants it in the garden. After some teasing monsters grab his last noo-noo, Marlon doesn't worry because he knows he'll have more on his noo-noo tree should he decide he needs one.

Making Connections

Setting aside comforting habits from infancy often marks that first step toward maturity. Some children adjust quickly to getting older. Others need to have reminders available. Marlon's gradual release of the pacifier, coupled with his back-up supply, demonstrates that letting go doesn't have to happen all at once.

Discussion Questions

- Did you use a pacifier or have a favorite blanket?
- What did you like about it?
- Do you have other favorites, such as a favorite stuffed animal?
- Adults also have favorites, such as a comfortable chair or special food. What favorites do your parents have?

No, David!

Shannon, David. 1998. *No, David!*
New York: Blue Sky.

Story Summary

As a young boy, author David Shannon created a book that was illustrated with drawings of him doing things he wasn't supposed to do. The text that accompanied that book—and that is found throughout this book illustrated with unique perspective drawings—are the words "No, David!" David got himself into all kinds of trouble: climbing on the kitchen chair to reach the cookie jar, tracking mud through the house, running naked through the neighborhood, playing with his food, and getting wild when it was time for bed. Children who seek to become more independent and frequently find themselves "doing the wrong thing" will appreciate knowing that, not only are they not the only children in the world who do such things, but are, just like David, loved by parents no matter what they do.

Making Connections

Growing up, and learning to do what is right, can be overwhelming for children who love to explore their world. Connecting with David and understanding that learning from your mistakes is a part of growing up will help children feel more comfortable in their world.

Discussion Questions

- What kinds of things have you done lately that got you into trouble?
- Can you think of some rules that you have in your house about the way you should behave?
- How can you learn from your mistakes?

Edward in Deep Water

Wells, Rosemary. 1995. *Edward in Deep Water*.
New York: Dial Books for Young Readers.

Story Summary

Edward is invited to his friend Georgina's birthday party, a party to be held at the local swimming pool. Looking forward to having fun with all the other children, and feeling brave, he takes only one of his two swim wings to the pool. To his dismay, his friends who no longer use any wings at all ridicule him. Despite their teasing, he prepares to go into the pool but discovers that his one wing has popped. Edward is accidentally pushed into the water, and thrashes about before the lifeguard rescues him. After his parents are called to pick him up early and take him home, Edward realizes he's not quite ready for a swimming party.

Making Connections

Learning the limitations of age and ability is a difficult but important realization for children. Reading this story will help them understand that not all children can do all things at the same age.

Discussion Questions

- Are there things your friends can do that you feel you can't do as well? What can you do to get better?

- What things would you like to try when you get older?

- Can you remember some things you were not able to do when you were younger that you can do now? How did you get better at those things?

Someone New

Zolotow, Charlotte. 1978. *Someone New.*
Illustrated by Erik Blegvad. New York: Harper & Row.

Story Summary

A young boy wakes up one morning feeling like someone is gone. His mom and dad and sister are there, but who is gone? The wallpaper he chose with blue and red balloons isn't as nice as it was last year, and he wishes he had chosen another one—but who is missing? Something is strange. His friend comes over to play, but all he wants to do is walk for a little while. He usually likes to play blocks with his sister, but not today. He just goes back to his room. Then he looks at all the things in his room and decides to get rid of many of them—but not all. He remembers things from last summer—and still feels strange, like his stuff belongs to someone else. He puts his things in a box and finally realizes someone's gone, someone's missing. He's in that box with all those things, and he is someone new.

Making Connections

Children are frequently aware of how their interests and friendships change. Talking about growing up, and how people change, will help a child better understand these confusing periods.

Discussion Questions

- Can you remember what you liked to do when you were younger?
- What are some of the new things you like to try now that you are older?
- What kinds of things do you think you'll do as you grow older?

CHAPTER 10

Homelessness

Fly Away Home
by Eve Bunting

The Lady in the Box
by Ann McGovern

I Can Hear the Sun
by Patricia Polacco

Home
*A Collaboration of Thirty Distinguished
Authors and Illustrators of Children's Books to
Aid the Homeless*
by Michael J. Rosen

Fly Away Home

Bunting, Eve. 1991. *Fly Away Home.*
Illustrated by Ronald Himler. New York: Clarion.

Story Summary

A young boy and his father live in the airport. They work at staying in the background, moving to different areas of the airport regularly, and sleeping while sitting up. They are careful to stay away from others who live there, minimizing their chances of being noticed. On the weekends the father takes a bus to work, and one of the other people watches the boy. Sometimes they earn money by returning rented luggage carts or carrying bags. The father and son save money, hoping to one day have a real home. Meanwhile they make the best of their situation, hoping for a better day.

Making Connections

Children who have never experienced homelessness find it difficult to understand. This simple story describes the efforts of people who are trying to survive with dignity. Readers will appreciate the basics, such as having their own bathroom or bed.

Discussion Questions

- Before reading the story, ask what an airport is like.
- What would it be like to live in an airport?
- After reading the story, ask what kinds of other problems someone might face when living in an airport.
- What other unusual places might have homeless people living in them?

The Lady in the Box

McGovern, Ann. 1997. *The Lady in the Box.*
Illustrated by Marni Backer. New York: Turtle Books.

Story Summary

Two young children notice a lady living in a box. Despite being told not to talk to strangers, they give her some food and a warm scarf. Soon the lady has to move from her warm spot because the deli owner doesn't want her near. When their mother questions them about the missing items, they tell her about the woman and how she had to move her box. Their mother talks with the woman and convinces the deli owner to let her have her warm place back. The children still want to help and volunteer at the neighborhood soup kitchen. Although the lady still lives in the box, the book ends with the hope that someday she will have a key to her own place.

Making Connections

Adults sometimes want to shield children from the harsh realities of homeless people who have been forced to live outside. The problem is so overwhelming that it may seem like one family can't help. This book presents a clear picture of one incident and how the children sought to help in a small way.

Discussion Questions

- Have you seen people living in boxes, under bridges, or on the street?
- How does seeing people living like this make you feel?
- What could you do to help someone while staying safe?
- What could adults do to help someone?

I Can Hear the Sun

Polacco, Patricia. 1996. *I Can Hear the Sun.*
New York: Philomel.

Story Summary

This modern myth is the story of a woman, Stephanie Michelle, who cares for animals and listens to the sun. When she befriends a young boy named Fondo she learns that he believes the geese have invited him to fly away with them. The other homeless people in the park become friends with him too, and as they grow closer, Fondo helps Stephanie Michelle feed the animals and do other chores throughout the park. Fondo never agrees to go home with Stephanie Michelle, despite her offers. He befriends a little blind goose and shares with his friends that the geese will be leaving soon, and that he will go with them. Before he is able to join the geese, however, he has to hide from people who want to place him in a permanent home. They give up their search for him, and the geese return so that Fondo can join them. He reminds Stephanie Michelle to always listen to the sun as he flies away with the geese.

Making Connections

Comprehending homelessness is difficult for children accustomed to the comforts found in a loving home. Discussing their feelings will help children begin to understand what it means to be homeless.

Discussion Questions

- Have you ever noticed someone you thought was homeless? How did it make you feel?
- What do you think you can do to help someone who is homeless?

Home
A Collaboration of Thirty Distinguished Authors and Illustrators of Children's Books to Aid the Homeless

Rosen, Michael J. 1992. *Home: A Collaboration of Thirty Distinguished Authors and Illustrators of Children's Books to Aid the Homeless.*
New York: HarperCollins.

Story Summary

This collection of short stories, poems, and essays celebrates various aspects of one's home: a stoop, a chair, things under the bed, a closet, and so forth. Each author gives a personal perspective on aspects that children and adults often take for granted. The book can be sampled or read in one or two sessions.

Making Connections

Although this book does not deal directly with the plight of the homeless, it supports Share Our Strength (SOS), a nonprofit organization for hunger relief. Children and adults can develop an appreciation for simple features of a home, such as a back porch and attic, in contrast to living in a box or under a bridge.

Discussion Questions

- What is your favorite part of your home?
- What would you miss most if you had to move?
- What would you want if you were homeless and were finally getting an apartment or home? A bed? A private bathroom? A window?
- The authors and illustrators have donated their royalties toward helping feed hungry people. How can you help?

CHAPTER 11
Illness

The Paper Chain
by Claire Blake, Eliza Blanchard,
and Kathy Parkinson

Rita Goes to the Hospital
by Martine Davison

When Molly Was in the Hospital
by Debbie Duncan

This Is a Hospital, Not a Zoo!
by Roberta Karim

The Lion Who Had Asthama
by Jonathan London

When Eric's Mom Fought Cancer
by Judith Vigna

The Paper Chain

Blake, Claire, Eliza Blanchard, and Kathy Parkinson. 1998.
The Paper Chain.
Illustrated by Kathy Parkinson. Santa Fe, N.M.: Health Press.

Story Summary

Marcus, his brother Ben, and their Mom and Dad love to play outside and do lots of fun things together, especially when the weather is warm. When they learn that Mom has to spend time in the hospital and have an operation for cancer, they try to cope with their feelings of sorrow and missing her, including making a paper chain to help them count the days until Mom comes home. Marcus and Ben learn about the follow-up treatments that she will have, including chemotherapy. Watching Mom lose her hair and feel tired all day is hard, but the family learns to adjust and discovers different ways to cope.

Making Connections

Watching a parent, other family member, or friend go through treatment for cancer can be frightening and confusing as children try to understand some of the physical and emotional changes patients go through. Explaining the unknown can help alleviate their fears and help them better understand what is happening.

Discussion Questions

- Do you have someone close to you who has gone through treatment for cancer? What changes did you notice about the way they looked?

- What changes did you notice about the way they acted?

- Can you think of things to help make them more comfortable?

Rita Goes to the Hospital

Davison, Martine. 1992. *Rita Goes to the Hospital.*
Illustrated by John Jones. New York: Random House.

Story Summary

Developed by the American Medical Society, *Rita Goes to the Hospital* tells the story of a young girl scheduled to have her tonsils removed. After Rita receives a letter from her doctor detailing her operation and she visits the hospital, she shares with her friend Maggie her fears and concerns. Rita takes a special tour of the hospital before her surgery and meets a friendly nurse, sees where she will put on her gown and slippers, and meets the anesthesiologist who will put her under before the surgery. She also tries on the hospital gowns with the doctor and nurses who are getting ready for work. Rita returns the next morning, feeling better about having her surgery, and is shown the inside of an operating room, including the monitors and other equipment that are used by the doctors during the surgery. When Rita awakens, she is taken to her room and sees the gifts left by her friends and family, gifts that make her feel a little better as she deals with her very sore throat. When Rita finally goes home, she and her mom stop at the store so Rita can pick out a new toy to make her feel a little better. The toy she chooses is a doctor's kit.

Making Connections

Many children experience a strong feeling of unease on their first visit to a hospital, especially when they are the patients. Providing them with information about what will happen and the people they will encounter will help to alleviate some of their fear.

Discussion Questions

- Can you think of some of the kinds of jobs people do in hospitals?
- Have you ever visited someone in the hospital? How did it make you feel?
- What kinds of happy things can you think of while you are in the hospital?

When Molly Was in the Hospital

Duncan, Debbie. 1994. *When Molly Was in the Hospital.*
Illustrated by Nina Ollikainen, M.D. Windsor, Calif.: Rayve Productions.

Story Summary

Anna remembers when her sister Molly went into the hospital, and when she first noticed that Molly was sick because she didn't want to play anymore and always wanted to be held. When Mom and Dad took Molly to the doctor he said she would have to have an operation. At the hospital Dad, Grandma, and Grandpa wait in the waiting room, and Mom and Anna walk around with a pager while Molly is having her operation. When the pager goes off they go to see Molly in her room, and all the tubes in Molly's nose and body frighten Anna. Anna misses her mom and dad while they are at the hospital with Molly, and she even thinks she is to blame for Molly getting sick. As Molly starts to get better she smiles and plays with Anna from her hospital bed, and after physical therapy she is finally allowed to come home.

Making Connections

Seeing a sibling or other young child gravely ill is often the first time children begin to understand their own vulnerability. Talking about their feelings and fears will help them better understand how to deal with those feelings.

Discussion Questions

- How did you feel when you first knew another child was sick?
- What kinds of things do you think you can do to help when a child is sick?

This Is a Hospital,
Not a Zoo!

Karim, Roberta. 1998. *This Is a Hospital, Not a Zoo!*
Illustrated by Sue Truesdell. New York: Clarion.

Story Summary

Filbert McKee has to stay in the hospital, and he is *not* happy about it. Faced with more shots, more tests, and lots of time in bed he relies on a "special delivery" of animal crackers to get through his days. When told to roll over so he can receive a shot, he turns into a rhino to scare the nurse away. When told to get into the cold wheelchair so he can be taken for his x-rays, he turns into a penguin and frightens his nurse. When told to take his medicine, he turns into a giraffe so the nurse can't reach his mouth. But with each change, Nurse Beluga explains he is in a hospital, not a zoo, and must do as he is told. Not until he meets with a doctor who understands his fear and concern does he feel better and safer about being in a hospital.

Making Connections

When a small child has to stay in the hospital, the number of people and vastness of the building contribute to the feelings of fright and confusion felt at having to be there because of an illness. Creating imaginary friends and characters, and finding a way to laugh despite the fear, can be strong and reassuring medicine.

Discussion Questions

- What do you think it would be like to stay at a hospital?
- Can you name some of the people at the hospital who are there to help you feel better?
- What special things would you take with you to make you feel better when you got scared?

The Lion
Who Had Asthma

London, Jonathan. 1992. *The Lion Who Had Asthma*.
Illustrated by Nadine Bernard Westcott. Morton Grove, Ill.: Albert Whitman.

Story Summary

Sean likes to play and imagines himself as many different creatures in the jungle. He imagines he's a lion, and roars in his jungle. He imagines he's a hippo splashing in the tub, and a giant munching trees at suppertime. But when he pretends to be a lion again, he begins to cough, his chest hurts, and it's hard for him to breathe—he remembers he has asthma. As he begins to wheeze and make a whistle sound when he breathes, he becomes frightened and starts to cry. With his family there to support him, he takes his treatment and imagines that the mask he wears is the mask of a pilot, swooping through the clouds. His treatment is over, his coughing has stopped, and he can land his plane and become the King of the Jungle again.

Making Connections

Serious illness in a child can lead to confusion and lots of questions of *why*? Through this story, children with asthma will be able to relate to the frustrations of another child and understand how illness can be treated.

Discussion Questions

- How do you feel about having asthma? Do you know anyone else who has asthma?
- How do you take care of your asthma?
- What are the many things you can do, even though you have asthma?

When Eric's Mom Fought Cancer

Vigna, Judith. 1993. *When Eric's Mom Fought Cancer.*
Morton Grove, Ill.: Albert Whitman.

Story Summary

Eric's mom has breast cancer and has been in the hospital a lot over the winter. So has Eric's dad, who spends time at the hospital and has yet to take Eric skiing with the new skis he got for Christmas. When his parents explained last fall that Mom was sick, Eric worried that she would die, even though the doctors told them they expect her to get better. She has to have a lot of operations, and her hair begins to fall out after she goes for treatments; she also feels sick and tired a lot, often unable to play with Eric. He gets frustrated when his mom doesn't pay attention to him, especially when he tries to do something special like a make a snowman for her. In anger he wrecks the snowman with his ski pole. Eric's grandmother tries to comfort him and make him feel better, but he doesn't really begin to feel better until the next day when Dad finally takes him skiing. While on their trip, Eric wonders aloud if a tight hug he gave his mom is the reason she is sick, or if he could get sick from being around her. Dad assures him Mom's illness is not his fault and that he can't catch cancer from her. A special hat purchased for Mom at the ski slope makes it look as though she has hair and brightens his day when she tells Eric she will wear it skiing the next year.

Making Connections

Watching a parent struggle with a grave illness is confusing, frightening, and frustrating for children who want to help but can't think of how. Explaining what is happening in simple yet comforting terms will allow children to begin to process their feelings.

Discussion Questions

- How does it make you feel when you see someone you love very sick?
- What do you think you can do to help that person feel better?

CHAPTER 12

Moving

**Marianthe's Story: Painted Words;
Marianthe's Story: Spoken Memories**
by Aliki

Good-bye, House
by Robin Ballard

I'm Not Moving, Mama!
by Nancy White Carlstrom

Go Away Monsters, Lickety Split!
by Nancy Evans Cooney

When Jessie Came Across the Sea
by Amy Hest

The New Boy
by Holly Keller

What You Know First
by Patricia MacLachlan

Lily
by Abigail Thomas

Marianthe's Story: Painted Words; Marianthe's Story: Spoken Memories

Aliki. 1998.
Marianthe's Story: Painted Words; Marianthe's Story: Spoken Memories.
New York: Greenwillow.

Story Summary

In the first story, Marianthe is going to a new school. She worries because she doesn't speak the language fluently. Gradually she begins to enjoy the activities, particularly the time at the easel. She begins to tell stories with her paintings. When a classmate teases her, she shows her pain through her painting. As she masters the language, she adds words to her paintings, giving the class her stories. In the second story, Marianthe tells the class about the war and famine that drove her family to emigrate. She describes the sadness felt at leaving her village. Her class begins to understand the challenges faced by people who have left their homes for a better life.

Making Connections

Many students come to the United States from other countries. It can be tempting for other students to tease them when they display cultural differences or have difficulty communicating. Understanding the courage of immigrants can help with the adjustment process.

Discussion Questions

- Are you or do you know someone who came from another country to live in the United States?

- What would it be like to live where you couldn't understand anything that was said to you?

- If you couldn't draw well like Marianthe, what could you do to communicate your feelings in a strange place?

- How can you help others who are new to the school or community?

Good-bye, House

Ballard, Robin. 1994. *Good-bye, House.*
New York: Greenwillow.

Story Summary

A young girl says good-bye to her house, one room and one memory at a time as she and her family prepare to move to a new house. The illustrations of the girl saying good-bye to all the things that are meaningful to her are accompanied by others that reflect her memories. This combination creates a visual journey of the girl's memories as she says good-bye to her room, the marks that indicated over the years how tall she was, her special play cupboard, her parents' room, the sewing closet where her mom made special clothes, and the trees and bushes she played around outside. Though she is sad to go, she realizes she will like her new home more when she meets a new friend.

Making Connections

Written in brief sentences with simple illustrations this book will be especially helpful for young children facing the prospect of moving to a new home.

Discussion Questions

- What will you miss about your old home?
- What things will you want to do at your new home?
- When you make new friends, what will you tell them about yourself?

I'm Not Moving, Mama!

Carlstrom, Nancy White. 1990. *I'm Not Moving, Mama!*
Illustrated by Thor Wickstrom. New York: Macmillan.

Story Summary

It's moving day, and Mama is doing the last-minute packing. One by one all of Mouse's favorite things get packed away, but he doesn't care because he's not moving. Mama packs his dinosaur and checkers, but it doesn't matter. He's going to sit by the window and watch the sun—but Mama says the sun is coming too. Mouse says he will hide, but Mama will find him. Mouse says she can take his toothbrush because he's not going—he'll look in the mirror and make funny faces. Mama says she hopes he comes because she couldn't make funny faces without him. On goes the list of things she can take, but Mama says many things will be in the new place, like birds, stars, climbing trees, and secret corners. Finally Mouse says he'll go, but he won't like it. Mama says she doesn't either, but the best part is she is not leaving Mouse behind. They'll remember all the things and be happy to be together in another place.

Making Connections

With the fear of moving to a new home comes the sadness of leaving an old house and neighborhood behind. Talking about memories to be taken from the old home and exciting things to do at a new one will help children better accept the change.

Discussion Questions

- What are your favorite things you can take to your new home?
- What special memories of your old home will you take with you?
- What are some special activities you want to do at your new home?

Go Away Monsters, Lickety Split!

Cooney, Nancy Evans. 1990. *Go Away Monsters, Lickety Split!*
Illustrated by Maxie Chambliss. New York: G. P. Putnam's Sons.

Story Summary

When Jeffrey and his family move into their new house, he helps unpack all the things they brought from his old house. Once he is comfortable that everything is in place in his new room, he helps get things put away outside, in the garage and the yard, learning all about the inside and outside of his new house. The first night in the new house he is so tired from all the work that he falls asleep in the middle of the floor. But the second night, as he tries to go to sleep in his room, he begins to notice how dark and quiet it is. Afraid of what he can't see, he runs to his parents' room for comfort, passing all the monsters of his imagination that might be lurking in the shadows. Over the course of the next two nights, his parents give him things to help him feel more comfortable in his new room, including a nightlight and flashlight so he can see. While these allow him to see a little better, they create more shadows that might still be hiding scary things. A visit from Grandma includes the gift of a kitten to keep Jeffrey company. Emboldened by his new friend, Jeffrey and the kitten explore the dark corners of his room, and Jeffrey becomes less afraid once he learns nothing scary lives in the shadows.

Making Connections

A child moving to a new home faces many of the same fears and worries faced by adults. This story helps children and adults begin to understand those feelings and how they can overcome their fears.

Discussion Questions

- What are your favorite things about your new house? What do you miss about your old house?
- Can you think of something you can do that will make you more comfortable in your new house?
- What can you do to your room to make it feel like it's your room?

When Jessie
Came Across the Sea

Hest, Amy. 1997. *When Jessie Came Across the Sea*.
Illustrated by P. J. Lynch. Cambridge, Mass.: Candlewick.

Story Summary

Jessie lives with her grandmother in a poor village. When the rabbi gets a ticket for someone to go to America, he chooses Jessie. On the long journey, she makes some friends and uses her sewing skills. After coming through Ellis Island, she faces her new life, writing to her grandmother about her new experiences. She continues to sew, saving her earnings to bring Grandmother to America. Her friend from the voyage renews their friendship, and they plan to marry. Finally, Grandmother begins her journey to America, and they anticipate a joyful wedding for Jessie.

Making Connections

Coming to America has often been seen as an irresistible opportunity, in spite of the hardships such an endeavor entails. This story illustrates the challenges and dedication shown by immigrants who were determined to find a new life.

Discussion Questions

- Do you think Jessie would have come to America if she hadn't been chosen?

- What do you think it would be like to leave behind your only family and go to a strange country?

- What skills do you think you could develop to help you make a living in a new country?

- How could you or your family help someone adjust to the United States?

The New Boy

Keller, Holly. 1991.
The New Boy. New York: Greenwillow.

Story Summary

When Milton, the new boy, arrives at school for his first day he sticks out his tongue at his classmates. When he hears that the other children have decided he is weird, he finds himself doing a lot of bad things. He messes the blocks, puts worms in lunch boxes, scares the teacher, sings during rest time, and doesn't share. The other kids tell him they think he is a bad boy, and he cries in his sadness. When he returns to school the next day he becomes almost too good, cleaning the erasers and making a mess, mixing too much paint, cleaning the turtle tank and letting the turtles out, and ignoring the whispers of the other kids during rest period. The other kids decide they liked it better when he was bad! Milton finally feels like a part of the class when another new boy arrives and begins to do many of the same bad things Milton used to do.

Making Connections

Children express their fears and anxiety in many ways, including "acting out" when faced with new situations. Talking about the changes and expectations will provide children an opportunity to face their fears more readily.

Discussion Questions

- What do you think a new school will be like?

- What kinds of things do you want to do in a new school?

- How do you think you can become friends with the students in a new school?

What You Know First

MacLachlan, Patricia. 1995. *What You Know First*.
Illustrated by Barry Moser. New York: HarperCollins.

Story Summary

A young girl contemplates telling her family that she won't move away from the farm to the ocean. She reminisces about the things that mean the most to her, such as the snow and the slough where the pipits feed. She thinks of relatives she could stay with, but she finally reconciles herself to leaving. She gathers her mementos so she won't forget her beloved prairie.

Making Connections

Moving to a new place can be exciting, but frightening. Finding the balance by taking along a few treasures helps this youngster ensure that she won't forget her past.

Discussion Questions

- How do you handle new places, homes, or communities?
- If you haven't moved yet, what would you do to help you remember your current home?
- What items could you put in a Memory Box to help you feel connected to the past?
- How can you help others know about the place you have left or are leaving?

Lily

Thomas, Abigail. 1994. *Lily*.
Illustrated by William Low. New York: Henry Holt.

Story Summary

Beautiful illustrations accompany the story of Lily the dog who, with Aunt Eliza, moves away from her very comfortable and cozy apartment in the city. Lily and Eliza have many special things that they do and places that they go, and she is very happy in her world. When the moving men come to take everything away she is very confused and sad. Everything is put into a box and nothing is where it is supposed to be, including her water bowl. Lily feels smaller and smaller as everything is carried out and the apartment becomes more sad and empty. When they get to their new home in Vermont, Lily at first feels very small and nervous in the soft grass, surrounded by lots of trees and new things to see. When all of their things are put away Lily is comforted by the fact that everything is in it's rightful spot again—just like Lily likes it.

Making Connections

The uncertainty of what lies ahead when children move can lead to anxious and fearful emotions. Highlighting the excitement of a new place while holding onto some of the comforts of an old home will help children through the transition.

Discussion Questions

- What are some of your favorite things that you will be taking to your new home?

- What are some new things you would like to try at your new home?

- What can you do to remember you old home and friends?

CHAPTER 13
Siblings

Nobody Asked Me If I Wanted a Baby Sister
by Martha G. Alexander

When the New Baby Comes, I'm Moving Out
by Martha G. Alexander

Monster Brother
by Mary Jane Auch

Mama, Coming and Going
by Judith Caseley

Waiting for Baby Joe
by Pat Lowery Collins

I Love You the Purplest
by Barbara M. Joosse

Peter's Chair
by Ezra Jack Keats

Geraldine's Baby Brother
by Holly Keller

Now I Will Never Leave the Dinner Table
by Jane Read Martin and Patricia Marx

Ellen and Penguin and the New Baby
by Clara Vulliamy

Nobody Asked Me
If I Wanted a Baby Sister

Alexander, Martha G. 1971. *Nobody Asked Me If I Wanted a Baby Sister*.
New York: Dial Press.

Story Summary

Oliver's new baby sister, Bonnie, arrives to much admiration and joy. But Oliver feels left out and a little bit neglected. Trying to get back his share of attention, he puts his sister in a wagon (gently laying her on pillows!) and tries to give her away to someone in his neighborhood. He asks everyone he sees if they want a baby; one couple shows him their triplets, saying they'll take the baby only if it's a boy. A man on the street says he'll take her if she can do tricks like his pets. Oliver's friend Toby agrees to take the baby, figuring she'll fit in at home since he already has so many brothers and sisters. When they get to Toby's, Bonnie doesn't stop crying until Oliver holds her. Realizing it might not be so bad to have a sister, Oliver begins to dream of playing games with his sister when she is older.

Making Connections

Older children often feel left out with the arrival of a new brother or sister as they realize they are not the sole focus of attention anymore. Understanding that a family's love can include more than one child will help siblings accept each new arrival.

Discussion Questions

- What are some special things you would like to do with the new baby?
- Are there some activities you would like to do that don't include the new baby?
- What makes you unique from your sibling?

When the New Baby Comes, I'm Moving Out

Alexander, Martha G. 1979. *When the New Baby Comes, I'm Moving Out.* New York: Dial Press. (Companion book to page 110)

Story Summary

Oliver notices his mom painting all "his things"—the high chair, the crib, even the spare bedroom. When she tells him she is getting ready for the new baby he gets angry because she didn't ask to borrow his things—Oliver needs them for a spaceship launch and for his wild animals. Mom tries to apologize, but Oliver points out that he can't even sit on her lap anymore! He tells her he wants to put the baby in a trash can, pound on it with a stick, take it to the dump, and leave her there. When Mom says that would be a terrible thing to do, Oliver decides she can stay, and he will go live outside in his tent. Mom tells Oliver how much she would miss him and wonders who will play hide and seek with her. Realizing the new baby won't be able to do these things, Oliver decides he'd better stay home after all, dreaming of all the special things he'll get to do with the baby.

Making Connections

A new baby in the family can be especially difficult for young children learning about having control in their lives. Highlighting those things they can still control will ease the transition for older siblings.

Discussion Questions

- What things and activities will you still do when the new baby arrives?
- What will you share with the new baby?
- What different feelings do you have about having a new brother or sister?

Monster Brother

Auch, Mary Jane. 1994. *Monster Brother.*
New York: Holiday House.

Story Summary

Rodney hates monsters, and despite everything he and his parents do to keep them out of his room they keep coming back. They make the room light, stinky, and really smelly, but the monsters keep coming. One day Mom tells Rodney he is going to have a new brother, but Rodney doesn't want one. At his aunt's wedding everyone talks about what the baby will look like, and Rodney imagines an ugly baby with all the worst features of his relatives. Rodney gets very nervous, until he dreams that the monsters run away because there are two children in the room, a dream that makes him anxious for his brother to arrive. Rodney and his mom look at old pictures of Rodney as a baby, thinking about what the new baby will look like. Rodney loves his new brother the minute he sees him but is worried he will be scared by the monsters. When he screams to scare the monsters his brother screams too—and between the two of them they scare the monsters away!

Making Connections

Often unable to figure out how to deal with the arrival of a new sibling, some children will develop fears in other areas—such as seeing monsters in the dark. Talking to children about the fear and confusion they may feel about a new baby will allow them to focus on those feelings rather than create other fears.

Discussion Questions

- How do you think things will change when the new baby arrives?
- What special things will you share with the new baby?
- What do you think the new baby will look like?

Mama, Coming and Going

Caseley, Judith. 1994. *Mama, Coming and Going.*
New York: Greenwillow.

Story Summary

In this delightfully illustrated book, big sister Jenna recalls the funny things Mama forgot to do after baby Mickey was born. She remembers to read Jenna books, but forgets to defrost the chicken for dinner—so they have pizza. She remembers Mickey's bathtime, but leaves the water running when someone comes to the door—so Jenna puts her boots on and goes wading. Mama tells Jenna she feels just like a chicken with its head cut off—and Jenna drew a picture of Mama with her head cut off. Mama forgets lots of other things—like not remembering who sent Mickey a new outfit when he was born. They even went to Albert's birthday party on the wrong day, but had cupcakes anyway because Mama appreciated the special help she got from Jenna.

Making Connections

All kinds of wonderful and strange things happen with the arrival of a new baby, and helping children realize that adults need to adjust too will help children understand the confusion they may feel.

Discussion Questions

- What kinds of things do you remember changing when your new baby came home?
- How can you help Mom with the new baby?

Waiting for Baby Joe

Collins, Pat Lowery. 1990. *Waiting for Baby Joe*.
Photographs by Joan Whinham Dunn. Niles, Ill.: Albert Whitman.

Story Summary

Missy and her family eagerly await the arrival of a new baby. Missy offers to let the baby have her old things and looks forward to when she can play with and hold the new baby. When her baby brother unexpectedly arrives two months early, Missy learns how premature babies are cared for and how they continue to grow in the hospital. She is able to visit her mother and baby brother in the hospital and is amazed at how small and different looking he is. When Mom comes home from the hospital without the baby there is tension in the house Missy isn't used to—everyone is worried about the baby and goes to the hospital a lot to visit him. One night, in frustration because she feels as if no one pays attention to her anymore, Missy hides under the piano where no one can find her. Her parents finally realize how difficult the situation has been for her, try to explain how hard it is for everyone, and share with her that things will be soon be fine. Though there are some scary moments when Joe finally comes home from the hospital, he begins to gain weight and strength and is loved and supported by the family—especially Missy.

Making Connections

The exciting buildup to the arrival of a new baby is quickly diminished when difficulties arise. Explaining to children what is happening and reminding them of their importance in the family will help them better deal with unexpected situations.

Discussion Questions

- How did you feel when you found out you were going to have a younger brother or sister?

- In what ways do you think you can help when the new baby is at home?

- What do you look forward to doing with the baby when he or she gets older?

I Love You the Purplest

Joosse, Barbara M. 1996. *I Love You the Purplest.*
Illustrated by Mary Whyte. San Francisco: Chronicle.

Story Summary

Two brothers go fishing with their mother. The boys compete on several levels. They wonder who has the most worms, and Mama points out that Max has the liveliest worms and Julian has the juiciest. Julian rows with the deepest strokes, while Max has the fastest strokes. When they want to know whom Mama loves best, she explains that she loves Julian the bluest and loves Max the reddest.

Making Connections

Feeling like a parent loves the other sibling better is a common emotion. Exploring a variety of expressions of love demonstrates how parents have the capacity to love every family member.

Discussion Questions

- Do you ever feel like your mother or father loves your sister or brother best?

- Do they ever feel that you are loved the best?

- Do you like different things about each of your friends?

- What do you like that's different about your parents, grandparents, brothers, or sisters?

Peter's Chair

Keats, Ezra Jack. 1967. *Peter's Chair*.
New York: Harper & Row.

Story Summary

Peter loves to play with his blocks and toys and build tall towers—but is frustrated when told he has to play more quietly because the baby is asleep. His new baby sister Susie has taken over all of his old, treasured things—his cradle and high chair were painted pink, and his crib was pink too. Before they have a chance to paint his little chair, however, Peter decides to run away, and takes some of his other treasured things as well. Once he arrives at his runaway spot, Peter realizes that he can no longer fit into his special chair because he has grown too big for it. He begins to realize how much he misses his family and eventually decides to go back home, offering to help paint his little chair pink for Susie.

Making Connections

Giving up attention from parents, room in the house, and treasured possessions are some of the difficulties encountered by children when they get a new brother or sister. Reading this story helps children cope with and understand how families may change, but the love remains strong.

Discussion Questions

- What kinds of things did you use as a baby that you no longer need?
- What things would you like your new brother or sister to be able to use?
- What are some of the special things you can still use?
- Can you think of some things your new brother or sister will need?

Geraldine's Baby Brother

Keller, Holly. 1994. *Geraldine's Baby Brother*.
New York: Greenwillow.

Story Summary

When Geraldine's baby brother is born, she feels as though no one pays attention to her anymore. The baby is always crying and her parents, grandmother, and aunt and uncle are always taking care of him. Even when her family makes an effort to comfort her she ignores them and refuses to eat with them. She tries to prove to them that she doesn't need them, and she gives herself a bath and puts herself to bed. One night, in the middle of the night, she hears her baby brother making noises in his crib. When she goes to check on him he not only doesn't cry, he does funny things that make her laugh! Geraldine decides to stay and read him stories and falls asleep in the chair, where Momma finds her the next morning.

Making Connections

Young children who are able to be a part of the preparation for a new baby and actively provide support will feel better about themselves and their new situation.

Discussion Questions

- What kinds of things would you like to do to help get ready for the new baby?
- What will you be able to help with when the new baby arrives?

Now I Will Never Leave the Dinner Table

Martin, Jane Read, and Patricia Marx. 1996.
Now I Will Never Leave the Dinner Table.
Illustrated by Roz Chast. New York: HarperCollins.

Story Summary

Patty Jane Pepper's big sister, Joy, is baby-sitting. Patty Jane puts her spinach in her pocket instead of eating it. Joy tells her she must stay until she eats one bite. Patty Jane describes how annoying her sister Joy is and fantasizes how life would be without her. Finally she contrives a way to make the spinach palatable and decides she wants Joy to stay in her life.

Making Connections

Resentment of an older sibling, especially when the sibling has power, can be a difficult emotion. Finding a balance in reacting to situations that arise can be helped through the fantasizing that Patty Jane experiences.

Discussion Questions

- Have you ever had an older sister or brother be in charge of you?

- Were you sometimes frustrated by it?

- Patty Jane decided that life without her sister wouldn't be all that great. What would you miss about your brother or sister?

- Did Patty Jane come up with a good solution to her problem?

Ellen and Penguin and the New Baby

Vulliamy, Clara. 1996. *Ellen and Penguin and the New Baby.*
Cambridge, Mass.: Candlewick.

Story Summary

When Ellen gets a new baby brother, she decides that her stuffed animal Penguin doesn't like him. The new baby cries a lot and has to go everywhere they go. He cries during a story, keeps Mom so busy she can't help make sure things don't go wrong (like paints spilling on the table), and even gets some of Ellen's old stuff that Penguin really likes. When Mom decides everyone needs a day out, they go to the park and visit all the different farm animals that live there. The baby starts to cry when they stop for a picnic lunch, and Mom and Ellen find they are unable to cheer him up with rattles or stories. The one thing that does calm the baby down is Penguin—who decides (along with Ellen) that babies aren't so bad after all.

Making Connections

Unable to express their own feelings, children will often use a cherished doll or stuffed animal to share their feelings for them. Allowing children to share those feelings will help them deal more readily with new situations.

Discussion Questions

- How did you feel when you found out you were going to have a new brother or sister?
- Are there ways you can think of to help make the new baby feel welcome?
- What are some special things you want to do with your parents after the baby arrives?

CHAPTER 14

Substance Abuse

I Wish Daddy Didn't Drink So Much
by Judith Vigna

My Big Sister Takes Drugs
by Judith Vigna

I Wish Daddy
Didn't Drink So Much

Vigna, Judith. 1988. *I Wish Daddy Didn't Drink So Much.*
Niles, Ill.: Albert Whitman.

Story Summary

After a disappointing Christmas, Lisa discovers new ways to deal with her father's alcoholism through the help of her mother and an older friend. Lisa observes that her dad "acts funny" when he drinks beer, and she wishes he wouldn't. He doesn't talk to her in the mornings and doesn't look at the Christmas card she made him. Mrs. Field is an older friend they invite for Christmas dinner whom they met at a meeting for people who have a lot of drinking in their family. She is the first person Lisa is allowed to talk to about her dad's drinking, but she is uninvited to Christmas dinner because Daddy is feeling sick. Lisa hopes her dad will take her sledding, as he promised, but he leaves the house in anger because there is no more beer. He falls when he gets home and gets mad at Lisa, making her wish she and her family could have a real Christmas like other people. When Lisa and her mom take the turkey to Mrs. Field's house for dinner, Mrs. Field shares with Lisa and her mom how she used to be with her children when she drank too much. The next day Lisa's daddy thanks her for the card and promises to take her sledding, and though she doesn't believe him, she realizes she has a friend in Mrs. Field.

Making Connections

When children observe the often-dramatic changes of an alcoholic adult they are confused and cannot understand why they hurt those around them. Encouraging children to talk about their feelings can make them feel less afraid and less alone in such a situation.

Discussion Questions

- Do you know someone who drinks a lot? In what way does he or she change while drinking?

- How does it make you feel to watch someone drink so much and change in those ways?

My Big Sister Takes Drugs

Vigna, Judith. 1990. *My Big Sister Takes Drugs.*
Niles, Ill.: Albert Whitman.

Story Summary

Paul's sister Tina made new friends last fall that Paul does not like. They are mean to him and tell him to get lost. Before the new friends came around, Paul was Tina's best friend. She used to walk him home from school and play with him but forgets about him now, especially when she skips school. New Year's Eve she tried to give him a pill, but Paul remembered that Mom and Dad said only to take pills with a doctor's permission. When Tina calls him a chicken he tells his parents about the incident. Grounded for a week, Tina tells Paul she will never play with him again. One evening, when Paul's new friend Jose is over for dinner, the police bring Tina home after finding her and her friends in the park smoking crack, something Paul learned about in school. When Paul is told he can't go to soccer camp with Jose because they need to use the money to send Tina to a special hospital to treat her drug problem, he gets very angry. When his mom explains how serious her problem is—and that she could die from it—he hopes she gets the help she needs. Tina finally comes home after her stay in the hospital, and though she has to go to a lot of meetings, she is Paul's friend once again.

Making Connections

Talking about the feelings a child has, when faced with substance abuse in a loved one, will help them to better understand what is happening and how they can be supportive.

Discussion Questions

- How does it make you feel to know someone you love is abusing drugs?

- What changes do you notice in that person?

- Do you have any ideas on how you can help that person stop abusing drugs?

CHAPTER 15

War

The Number on My Grandfather's Arm
by David Adler

Sweet Dried Apples
A Vietnamese Wartime Childhood
by Rosemary Breckler

The Blue and the Gray
by Eve Bunting

The Wall
by Eve Bunting

The Number on My Grandfather's Arm

Adler, David. 1987. *The Number on My Grandfather's Arm.*
Photographs by Rose Eichenbaum.
New York: Union of American Hebrew Congregations Press.

Story Summary

A young girl's grandfather, a tailor who fixes her clothes when they rip or tear, comes to dinner with her family and to stay with her while her parents go out. He always wears ties and long-sleeved shirts, and while they are doing the dishes she asks about the numbers on his arm she has never seen before. He explains that he grew up in a small village in Eastern Europe, in the mountains where they had no cars and traveled by horse and wagon. He also describes what life was like in Poland for Jews and the things the Nazis did to them because they were Jewish. Telling her about Adolf Hitler, he tells her about the yellow stars they were forced to wear and the persecution of the Jews. He also explains Hitler's plan to kill the Jews, describes the concentration camp where the numbers were tattooed onto his arm, and explains that the Nazis killed 6 million people. The girl and her grandfather, with tears in his eyes, sit quietly for a while; she tells him that he shouldn't be ashamed to let people see his arm—he didn't do anything wrong and that the Nazis should be ashamed. With hugs and a smile, they return to the dishes with rolled up sleeves.

Making Connections

Understanding the grimness of war is difficult for young children, especially when learning of the horrors inflicted on its victims. Discussing what happened and how people learned to cope can lessen the confusion.

Discussion Questions

- Do you know someone who was affected by a war?
- How does it make you feel?
- What can you do to help someone who was involved in a war?

Sweet Dried Apples
A Vietnamese Wartime Childhood
Breckler, Rosemary. 1996.
Sweet Dried Apples: A Vietnamese Wartime Childhood.
Illustrated by Deborah Kogan Ray. Boston: Houghton Mifflin.

Story Summary

A young girl misses her father who has joined the army. Her grandfather, the village herb doctor, watches over her and her brother. But after he takes a journey, he returns in poor health, advising them to hide. Fire from the war destroys their community, and Grandfather dies. The children and their mother flee the country, and the young girl hopes to one day return to honor her lost grandfather.

Making Connections

The realities of war, experienced by so many immigrants in the United States, are told with simplicity in this beautifully illustrated story. Readers will recognize the efforts to maintain a normal life in spite of the war, while acknowledging the horrors people face.

Discussion Questions

- Do you know people who have fought in a war?

- What are their thoughts about their experiences? Will they talk about what happened?

- How did the children try to find joy in spite of their situation?

- How would you find the courage to keep your life going during war and then eventually leave your home?

The Blue and the Gray

Bunting, Eve. 1996. *The Blue and the Gray.*
Illustrated by Ned Bittinger. New York: Scholastic.

Story Summary

A father tells his son and friend about the battle that was fought near their homes during the Civil War. They discuss how a Northern general and a Southern captain lost their friendship on the ridge. The boys ponder how friends and brothers could fight and die during the war. Although no monument marks the battle site, the boys decide to keep alive the memory of those who died.

Making Connections

Children may find it difficult to understand how best friends or family members can end up as enemies during a war. These gentle descriptions of the challenges of war remind readers of the importance of remembering those who fought and died for their beliefs.

Discussion Questions

- Have you ever had a fight with your best friend? Did you make up?
- Do you know people who have fought in a war?
- Why do you think whole groups of people or countries fight?
- What can you do to help stop people from fighting?
- What do you do to stop a fight with people you love?

The Wall

Bunting, Eve. 1990. *The Wall.*
Illustrated by Ronald Himler. New York: Clarion.

Story Summary

A little boy and his father visit the Vietnam War Memorial in Washington, D.C., searching for the name of the little boy's grandpa engraved on the stone. They see other people looking too, including a man with no legs who sits in a wheelchair. People have left mementos, like pictures and flags and teddy bears, and others also come to search for names. When at last they find the name they are looking for, the little boy and his dad touch the name and make a rubbing of it with the paper and pencil they brought to take home. People come and go as the boy and his father stand quietly together in front of the wall, remembering the men and women who died in the war.

Making Connections

For most children, war is something very far away and unfamiliar. But for others, it is very personal if they have experienced it or lost a family member. Understanding one way of remembering and coping, depicted through this story, may bring a sense of comfort to some children.

Discussion Questions

- What do you think happens in a war? Who have you known who died in a war?

- How do you feel about war? What would you like to know about it?

- What are some other things we can do to remember people who died in a war?

Bibliography

Adler, David. 1987. *The Number on My Grandfather's Arm*. Photographs by Rose Eichenbaum. New York: Union of American Hebrew Congregations Press.

Alexander, Martha G. 1971. *Nobody Asked Me If I Wanted a Baby Sister*. New York: Dial Press.

———. 1979. *When the New Baby Comes, I'm Moving Out*. New York: Dial Press. (Companion book to above.)

Aliki. 1998. *Marianthe's Story: Painted Words; Marianthe's Story: Spoken Memories*. New York: Greenwillow.

Allan, Nicholas. 1996. *Heaven*. New York: HarperCollins.

Arkin, Alan. 1994. *Some Fine Grampa!* Illustrated by Dirk Zimmer. New York: HarperCollins.

Auch, Mary Jane. 1994. *Monster Brother*. New York: Holiday House.

Bahr, Mary. 1992. *The Memory Box*. Illustrated by David Cunningham. Morton Grove, Ill.: Albert Whitman.

Bailey, Debbie. 1998. *My Family*. Photographs by Susan Huszar. Willowdale, Ontario: Annick.

Ballard, Robin. 1994. *Good-bye, House*. New York: Greenwillow.

Blake, Claire, Eliza Blanchard, and Kathy Parkinson. 1998. *The Paper Chain*. Illustrated by Kathy Parkinson. Santa Fe, N.M.: Health Press.

Blatchford, Claire H. 1998. *Going with the Flow*. Illustrated by Janice Lee Porter. Minneapolis, Minn.: Carolrhoda.

Bloom, Suzanne. 1991. *A Family for Jamie: An Adoption Story*. New York: Crown.

Blumenthal, Deborah. 1996. *The Chocolate-Covered-Cookie Tantrum*. Illustrated by Harvey Stevenson. New York: Clarion.

Booth, Barbara D. 1991. *Mandy*. Illustrated by Jim LaMarche. New York: Lothrop, Lee & Shepard.

Breckler, Rosemary. 1996. *Sweet Dried Apples: A Vietnamese Wartime Childhood*. Illustrated by Deborah Kogan Ray. Boston: Houghton Mifflin.

Brillhart, Julie. 1990. *Anna's Goodbye Apron*. Niles, Ill.: Albert Whitman.

Buehner, Caralyn. 1998. *I Did It, I'm Sorry*. Illustrated by Mark Buehner. New York: Dial Books for Young Readers.

Bunting, Eve. 1990. *The Wall*. Illustrated by Ronald Himler. New York: Clarion.

———. 1991. *Fly Away Home*. Illustrated by Ronald Himler. New York: Clarion.

———. 1993. *Someday a Tree*. Illustrated by Ronald Himler. New York: Clarion.

———. 1996. *The Blue and the Gray*. Illustrated by Ned Bittinger. New York: Scholastic.

———. 1997. *Twinnies*. Illustrated by Nancy Carpenter. San Diego, Calif.: Harcourt Brace.

Caines, Jeannette Franklin. 1986. *Chilly Stomach*. Illustrated by Pat Cummings. New York: Harper & Row.

Carlson, Nancy L. 1988. *Arnie Goes to Camp*. New York: Viking Kestrel.

———. 1990. *Arnie and the New Kid*. New York: Viking.

Carlstrom, Nancy White. 1990. *I'm Not Moving, Mama!* Illustrated by Thor Wickstrom. New York: Macmillan.

Carmichael, Clay. 1998. *Used-Up Bear*. New York: North-South Books.

Carrick, Carol. 1988. *Left Behind*. Illustrated by Donald Carrick. New York: Clarion.

Carter, Dorothy. 1998. *Bye, Mis' Lela*. Illustrated by Harvey Stevenson. New York: Farrar, Straus & Giroux.

Caseley, Judith. 1994. *Mama, Coming and Going*. New York: Greenwillow.

Clement, Rod. 1997. *Grandpa's Teeth*. New York: HarperCollins.

Colli, Monica. 1992. *Twins*. Illustrated by Filippo Brunello. New York: Child's Play (Ltd.).

Collins, Pat Lowery. 1990. *Waiting for Baby Joe*. Photographs by Joan Whinham Dunn. Niles, Ill.: Albert Whitman.

Cooney, Nancy Evans. 1990. *Go Away Monsters, Lickety Split!* Illustrated by Maxie Chambliss. New York: G. P. Putnam's Sons.

Curtis, Jamie Lee. 1996. *Tell Me Again About the Night I Was Born*. Illustrated by Laura Cornell. New York: HarperCollins.

———. 1998. *Today I Feel Silly & Other Moods That Make My Day*. Illustrated by Laura Cornell. New York: HarperCollins.

Damrell, Liz. 1991. *With the Wind*. Illustrated by Stephen Marchesi. New York: Orchard.

Davison, Martine. 1992. *Rita Goes to the Hospital*. Illustrated by John Jones. New York: Random House.

dePaola, Tomie. 1973. *Nana Upstairs & Nana Downstairs*. New York: G. P. Putnam's Sons.

Drescher, Joan. 1986. *My Mother's Getting Married*. New York: Dial Books for Young Readers.

Duncan, Debbie. 1994. *When Molly Was in the Hospital*. Illustrated by Nina Ollikainen, M.D. Windsor, Calif.: Rayve Productions.

Edwards, Pamela Duncan. 1998. *The Grumpy Morning*. Illustrated by Darcia Labrosse. New York: Hyperion Books for Children.

Fleming, Virginia. 1993. *Be Good to Eddie Lee*. Illustrated by Floyd Cooper. New York: Philomel Books.

Fowler, Susie Gregg. 1998. *Beautiful*. Illustrated by Jim Fowler. New York: Greenwillow.

Hest, Amy. 1996. *Baby Duck and the Bad Eyeglasses*. Illustrated by Jill Barton. Cambridge, Mass.: Candlewick.

———. 1997. *When Jessie Came Across the Sea*. Illustrated by P. J. Lynch. Cambridge, Mass.: Candlewick.

Hines, Anna Grossnickle. 1998. *My Own Big Bed*. Illustrated by Mary Watson. New York: Greenwillow.

Hoffman, Mary. 1995. *Boundless Grace*. Illustrated by Caroline Binch. New York: Dial Books for Young Readers.

Jeram, Anita. 1995. *Daisy Dare*. Cambridge, Mass.: Candlewick.

Joosse, Barbara M. 1996. *I Love You the Purplest*. Illustrated by Mary Whyte. San Francisco: Chronicle.

Kamish, Daniel, and David Kamish. 1998. *The Night the Scary Beasties Popped Out of My Head*. New York: Random House.

Karim, Roberta. 1998. *This Is a Hospital, Not a Zoo!* Illustrated by Sue Truesdell. New York: Clarion.

Kasza, Keiko. 1992. *A Mother for Choco*. New York: Putnam.

Keats, Ezra Jack. 1967. *Peter's Chair*. New York: Harper & Row.

Keller, Holly. 1991. *The New Boy*. New York: Greenwillow.

———. 1994. *Geraldine's Baby Brother*. New York: Greenwillow.

Koehler, Phoebe. 1990. *The Day We Met You*. New York: Bradbury.

———. 1993. *Making Room*. New York: Bradbury.

Krause, Robert. 1998. *Little Louie the Baby Bloomer.* Illustrated by Jose Aruego and Ariane Dewey. New York: HarperCollins.

Kvasnosky, Laura McGee. 1998. *Zelda and Ivy.* Cambridge, Mass.: Candlewick.

Levete, Sarah. 1998. *How Do I Feel About Looking After Myself.* Brookfield, Conn.: Copper Beech.

———. 1998. *How Do I Feel About Making Friends.* Brookfield, Conn.: Copper Beech.

London, Jonathan. 1992. *The Lion Who Had Asthma.* Illustrated by Nadine Bernard Westcott. Morton Grove, Ill.: Albert Whitman.

Lowery, Linda. 1994. *Laurie Tells.* Illustrated by John Eric Karpinski. Minneapolis, Minn.: Carolrhoda.

MacLachlan, Patricia. 1995. *What You Know First.* Illustrated by Barry Moser. New York: HarperCollins.

Martin, Jane Read, and Patricia Marx. 1996. *Now I Will Never Leave the Dinner Table.* Illustrated by Roz Chast. New York: HarperCollins.

McGovern, Ann. 1997. *The Lady in the Box.* Illustrated by Marni Backer. New York: Turtle Books.

Miller, Kathryn Ann. 1994. *Did My First Mother Love Me? A Story for an Adopted Child.* Illustrated by Jami Moffett. Buena Park, Calif.: Morning Glory.

Moran, George. 1995. *Imagine Me on a Sit-Ski!* Illustrated by Nadine Bernard Westcott. Morton Grove, Ill.: Albert Whitman.

Murphy, Jill. 1995. *The Last Noo-Noo.* Cambridge, Mass.: Candlewick.

Oram, Hiawyn. 1998. *Badger's Bad Mood.* Illustrated by Susan Varley. New York: Arthur A. Levine.

Polacco, Patricia. 1990. *Thundercake.* New York: Philomel.

———. 1996. *I Can Hear the Sun.* New York: Philomel.

Powell, E. Sandy. 1991. *Daisy.* Illustrated by Peter J. Thornton. Minneapolis, Minn.: Carolrhoda.

Rabe, Berniece. 1988. *Where's Chimpy?* Photographs by Diane Schmidt. Niles, Ill.: Albert Whitman.

Rau, Dana Meachen. 1998. *The Secret Code.* Illustrated by Bari Weissman. New York: Children's Press.

Root, Phyllis. 1996. *Contrary Bear.* Illustrated by Laura Cornell. New York: HarperCollins.

Rosen, Michael J. 1992. *Home: A Collaboration of Thirty Distinguished Authors and Illustrators of Children's Books to Aid the Homeless*. New York: HarperCollins.

Russo, Marisabina. 1992. *Alex is My Friend*. New York: Greenwillow.

Schecter, Ben. 1996. *Great-Uncle Alfred Forgets*. New York: HarperCollins.

Scheller, Melanie. 1992. *My Grandfather's Hat*. Illustrated by Keiko Narahashi. New York: Maxwell Macmillan International.

Senisi, Ellen B. 1998. *Just Kids: Visiting a Class for Children with Special Needs*. New York: Dutton Children's Books.

Shange, Ntozake. 1977. *Whitewash*. Illustrated by Michael Sporn. New York: Walker.

Shannon, David. 1998. *No, David!* New York: Blue Sky.

Smalls, Irene. 1996. *Beginning School*. Illustrated by Toni Goffe. Parsippany, N.J.: Silver Burdett Press.

Snihura, Ulana. 1998. *I Miss Franklin P. Shuckles*. Illustrations by Leanne Franson. Toronto: Annick.

Snyder, Carol. 1994. *One Up, One Down*. Illustrated by Maxie Chambliss. New York: Atheneum.

Thomas, Abigail. 1994. *Lily*. Illustrated by William Low. New York: Henry Holt.

Thomas, Jane Resh. 1988. *Saying Good-bye to Grandma*. Illustrated by Marcia Sewall. New York: Clarion.

Thomas, Shelley Moore. 1998. *Somewhere Today: A Book of Peace*. Photographs by Eric Futran. Morton Grove, Ill.: Albert Whitman.

Thompson, Mary. 1992. *My Brother Matthew*. New York: Woodbine House.

Vigna, Judith. 1988. *I Wish Daddy Didn't Drink So Much*. Niles, Ill.: Albert Whitman.

———. 1990. *My Big Sister Takes Drugs*. Niles, Ill.: Albert Whitman.

———. 1991. *Saying Goodbye to Daddy*. Morton Grove, Ill.: Albert Whitman.

———. 1993. *When Eric's Mom Fought Cancer*. Morton Grove, Ill.: Albert Whitman.

———. 1995. *My Two Uncles*. Morton Grove, Ill.: Albert Whitman.

Vulliamy, Clara. 1996. *Ellen and Penguin and the New Baby*. Cambridge, Mass.: Candlewick.

Wahl, Mats. 1990. *Grandfather's Laika*. Illustrated by Tord Nygren. Minneapolis, Minn.: Carolrhoda.

Walter, Mildred Pitts. 1995. *Darkness*. Illustrated by Marcia Jameson. New York: Simon & Schuster.

Wells, Rosemary. 1995. *Edward in Deep Water*. New York: Dial Books for Young Readers.

Willhoite, Michael. 1990. *Daddy's Roommate*. Boston, Mass.: Alyson Wonderland.

Zolotow, Charlotte. 1978. *Someone New*. Illustrated by Erik Blegvad. New York: Harper & Row.

———. 1995. *The Old Dog*. Illustrated by James Ransome. New York: HarperCollins.

———. 1997. *Who Is Ben?* Illustrated by Kathryn Jacobi. New York: HarperCollins.

Index of Authors

Index of Titles